The Glory

REV. DR. WILLIAM J. SCHECK

PAPER TIGERS PUBLISHING

Paper Tigers Publishing, Inc.
Mr. Jonathan A. Lewis, Publisher
9625 Boylagh Ave.
Las Vegas, Nevada, USA 89129-7852
702–696–9808
info@papertigers.cc
www.papertigers.cc

To report errors, please contact support@papertigers.cc

First Edition

Copyright Registration
United States of America
TXu 977-814

ISBN 0-9719339-3-6

Printed and bound in the United States of America

THE GLORY

METHODS TO BECOME ONE WITH GOD, A MANUAL FOR MIRACLES & PALSM [POEMS]

REV. DR. WILLIAM J. SCHECK

DEDICATION

This book is dedicated to GOD [ATUM], the GOD within you, the GOD THAT IS YOU! When you read this book and the palms [poems] and you will know that these writings were meant for you to help you find GOD. It is my hope that in some way you will be inspired by what you read to dedicate your life to be in one with GOD; and perhaps, this book and the palms will help you to find this path.

When you find GOD [ATUM] you are reborn in the Mind of GOD; and you are on your new earth journey to the GOD within you, without you, and the GOD that encompass you and which you are apart. This is your path, one which only you know, not me. It is a path that only you can walk, not me! Perhaps, what you read your will help you to get there. Being there is something that only you will know. It will be your a unique experience, your unique path to GOD [ATUM}. When you obtain it, only you will know and it only really matters to you. Some may notice you are entirely different. Others may notice no change whatsoever. But, it doesn't matter because you know you have found GOD [ATUM].

The most important thing is to try to be one with your GOD! That is the GOD within you, the GOD without you, and the GOD encompassing you in LOVE! So, this book and palms are dedicated to you, GOD, and all those who realize that the Mind of GOD has created all of this and we are apart of GOD'S Mind and LOVE!

Table of Contents

INTRODUCTION:
. THE GLORY: METHODS TO BECOME ONE WITH GOD, A MANUAL FOR MIRACLES & PALSM [POEMS]

Here it is the Glory of God! That is we all want to become one with God and be with God in all things, but many of us have no understanding of the paths to being one with God.

Consequently, we struggle and perhaps we only become one with God upon the death of our physically bodies. We are born and we die and we fill up the in-between with many things, but we all are seekers of God whether we realize it or not.

This book is in part a methodology for finding God within you and without you for God is in all things. God is the original thought, The All. For, God is the infinite living mind the creator of all there is and we can be co-creators with The All, with God. The second section of this book is a manual for the creation of miracles. Once we find God, it is up tous to co-create with God the miracles, which makes our existence while in the earth dimension beauty and full of loving-kindness. To cure our minds and bodies the best we can in order that we may appreciate the beauty of God's earth with the full realization that we will eventually pass into another dimension in order to continue our journey to becoming completely one with God.

The third section of this book contains poems, which are my poems co-created with THE ALL. They are special to me, and I hope you will find meaning in them in a special way for you that is in your essence.

We are here on earth to experience the beauty of God's earth creations to the fullest. As you journey through this book, I hope that you find the beauty of God and you experience a oneness with God through co-creating with God.us to co-create with God the miracles, which makes our existence while in the earth dimension beauty and full of loving-kindness. To cure our minds and bodies the best we can in order that we may appreciate the beauty of God's earth with the full realization that we will eventually pass into another dimension in order to continue our journey to becoming completely one with God.

BOOK 1
CHAPTER 1
INTRODUCTION

The story of mankind has always been that of a spiritual quest known or unknown. Man has always been in search of his Soul and in search of God. How God and the Soul are found has taken many different paths. Some of these paths have been extreme and full of great difficulties and many people have met with failure and never found their Soul and God. Other paths have been easier, but not know to most of mankind. For the path to God and the Soul is within and without us - you and it is not difficult to find it if we clear our minds and become seekers of the God within and without for all around is the Soul and the universal God of love and kindness.

This is the story of the various paths to Soul and God and what happens to us as we follow these paths and how our metaphysical experiences bring us closer to God within and without and our Souls and the story of the miracles which occur on the way to finding God within and without.

As we approach these different methods perhaps a synthesis will occur for you the seeker and you will find your own personal path to God.

Seeking the Soul and God should not be a difficult task because God wants us to be one with God but because man has free will mankind has made this task difficult and perhaps this is the time to make this task of finding the Soul and God within and without much easier.

During this path to the Soul and God, we will study various methods of seeking offered to us from the mystical masters some known and others unknown. First, there is the path offered by Jesus the CHRIST and THE BIBLE [The BOOK], then Buddha and selections from the lesser known mystical masters but perhaps the more profound and through these mystical master we will learn how to create miracles within us and for others and in your seeking may you always know that the loving kindness of God is always with you.

CHAPTER II

JESUS - THE CHRIST - THE BIBLE [The Book]

When I was a child, I did not know it, but I met Jesus the Christ within me for I was that Christ and so were you. This was the time when I was a pure Soul - the God within Soul. However, I did not have the capacity to keep this pure God within me and this is the story of the "Law of God and the Law of Man". God's law is that of love and God is all. Love is the nature of God; Law is the way God works or the action of God. It is the area of Law, God in Action, that all the mystery lies. [Addington 1996, 48] The great Law, which encompasses all law on the mental and physical level, is the law of cause and effect [karma]. The first cause or divine law is God. The principal is always the same. The first cause is love and love begets love. The Law is the Law of Love and divine right action, the law that transcends all other laws. When you and I were children we lived by this Law, we were pure, we were the Christ. However, man was given the power of choice and has the power to entertain what thoughts he brings into his mind and in addition every though in our minds produces an effect. Since man can chose the types of thought which will have an undesirable effect in his life, he is them free to part company with his Creator [the universal God within and without] and the perfect plan provided for him. God cannot compel man to enjoy the Bliss that he could enjoy were he to keep his thoughts God-Centered. [Addington 1996, 49]

The Bible is an important story because it tells us how we lost being centered with God and how we can become centered with God but it is a hard and difficult journey for most who read The Bible because they do not understand its true metaphysical meaning and they rarely obtain enlightenment. Perhaps if they chose another approach to the reading and understanding of the Bible, they will obtain union with God and their Soul again.

The Bible is has both outer and inner meaning. However, it is the inner meaning of The Bible, which is the most important to helping us find our spiritual path. "The Bible is one of the finest examples of the use of allegorical writing." [Addington 1996, 12] Often times the outer meanings of the stories do not make sense and they leave the reader confused which is the reason so many people turn away from The Bible because it does not make sense to them. [Addington 1996, 12] To understand The Bible, we must look for the inner meaning, that is the esoteric!

The story of the Garden of Eden when interpreted from its outer meaning that is esoteric does not make sense because science has proven that man has existed for thousand of years, not just 4,000 years.

The outer meaning will always leave us confused, but the inner meaning holds together, proves itself with accuracy and precision. The Garden of Eden Story is pure allegory with a deep and wonderful esoteric meaning. And so we find in the Garden of Eden allegory: "to eat" means to make one's own, to partake of mentally. Today the Adam and Eve of each of us must chose whether "to eat" from the "tree of life", which means to partake in the truth about God and man in the garden of the soul, the kingdom of God within, called the "Garden of Eden" in The Bible, or whether we shall "eat" from the "tree of knowledge of good and evil", our own false judgment in judging by appearances. [Addington 1996, 13-14]

This story of Adam and Eve in the Garden of Eden can be used a beautiful mediation which can bring us to enlightenment if we understands the inner meaning of the story which is to find God within that is the truth that God is within us and always there, but we lose this feeling for God and the GOD-US when we begin to make judgments concerning the appearances of the world when we become seekers of knowledge based on judgments which create attachments leading to pain and suffering. This story is meant to lead us to the path to God within and to guide us away from illusions of judgments, attachments, pain and suffering. By understanding this story from The Bible and others similar stories found in The Bible, we can be guided to finding God within and our GOD-SELF. The inner meaning of The Bible is our guide to immediate enlightenment to the God within *THE TREE OF LIFE*.

To understand The Bible we must have an understanding of the people who wrote The Bible. They were Orientals and their minds approach things differently than the Occidental mind. The Orientals are use to thinking in what we would call "double talk", that is saying one thing but knowing underneath lies a rich, hidden meaning. [Addington 1996, 15]

Thus, *to go up into the mountain*, an expression that is often found in both the Old and New Testaments, is to go into a higher state of spiritual consciousness. *To go to the desert or the wilderness* is to go into the

wildness of unenlightened or arid though. The streams in the desert are streams of living water, streams of Truth, making the desert "blossom as the rose," making the conscious beautiful. To "enlarge thy border' is to expand the borders of Nome's own limited or temporary consciousness. The Bible is actually its own best interpreter and somewhere or other in this magnificent book, all of these terms are qualified. [Addington 1996, 15]

The Eastern mind expresses spiritual truths as allegory or parable. The result is on the surface you may see in The Bible a picture of creed, a morale rule of conduct, great battles, romance, violence, famines, intrigue, but there is a more spiritual inner meaning. [Addington 1996, 16] When you discover this meaning, *THE WORD OF GOD,* then you can experience immediate enlightenment because GOD'S word becomes your inner voice and you are one with GOD within. The word of GOD is *LOVE!* If you mediate on LOVE, then you hear the word of GOD within and you are one with GOD and you are immediately enlightened.

"God is love and God is all. Love is the nature of God; Law is the way God works or the action of God. It is in the area of Law. God in action, that all the mystery lies." [Addington 1996, 48] The great Law which encompasses all is the law of cause and effect. "The First Cause is God or Divine Love. The First Cause is Love and Love begets love. The divine Law is the Law of Love and divine right action, the Law that transcends all other laws." [Addington 1996, 48] Consequently, every thought produces an effect. Thoughts are energy, which produce an effect. Mediations on Love will open the God spirit within and you will become one with GOD for God is LOVE. We all can enjoy our *BLISS* if we can keep our thoughts God centered at all times, that is centered on *LOVE.*

In the beginning God created the heaven and the earth. [Genesis 1:1]

In the beginning there is nothing but God, for God is all there is. Everything created by God must be created from God. God is the only substance. [Addington 1996, 55]

The heaven and earth refer to the creative process. As within, so without. The heaven is the consciousness within; it is out-pictured as the form, the earth or that part that shows. The invisible becomes the visible. [Addington 1996, 53]

> And the earth was without form, and void; and darkness
> was upon the face of the deep. And the Sprit of God
> moved upon the face of the waters. And God said, Let
> there be light: and there was light. [Genesis 1:2,3]

God moves within man to create the without the earth, and God in man as man accomplishes GOD'S great creative work. God's creative spirit moves man. [Addington 1996, 54] It is God's spirit of *LOVE* that moves man to become one with God and all of mankind.

Then, on the sixth day God made man in God's image. God created the male [wisdom, direct mind] and the female [love, subjective mind], the yin and the yang. God created wisdom and love, which are the parent of spiritual man/woman. Spiritual man/woman is the offspring, the image of this Father Creator, God. Spiritual man/woman is created out of the very essence of God. God and spiritual man/woman our one. [Addington 1996, 57] We are one with God and perfect. To be with God we can mediate that we are *LOVE, WE ARE ONE WITH GOD, WE ARE PREFECT, FOR WE ARE GOD.*

When we speak the WORD of GOD, which is LOVE, the CHRIST within us, then we understand creation for

> In the beginning was the Word, the Word was with
> God, and the Word was God.
>
> The same was in the beginning with God.
>
> All things were made by him; and without him was not
> any thing that was made.
>
> In him was life; and the life was the light of men.
>
> And the light shineth in darkness; and the darkness
> comprehend it not.
>
> And the Word was made flesh, and dwelt among us,
> (and we behold his glory, the glory as of the only
> begotten of the Father, full of grace and truth. [St.
> John 1:1-5,14]

The Bible *[GOD]* is ***TEACHING*** us that all of life comes through light [wisdom and understanding] that everything is created by God out of Himself. The Christ is the spirit of God within us. Through the Christ within us, we have the essence of Love Itself - love and wisdom. Jesus was the word made Flesh - the living God as we all are. Jesus [Man/Woman] - God was made flesh to explain to us that by living by grace is living in the Garden of Eden. That is we should not make comparisons this is good and that is evil. We should not trust our mental powers and material things instead of the Spirit [God within] for they will only bring forth sorrow "all the days of thy life". We live in the Garden of Eden if we live intuitively from the inside out or with God within. Jesus said, "the kingdom of heaven is at hand." The "Kingdom of heaven" and the "Garden of Eden" are one and the same. Jesus accepted the Old Testament teaching of one God, " the Lord, our God, is one Lord" - and to Love God with all they mind and understanding, with your total self. Jesus taught that duality was destructive, bringing sorrow and pain, that we should love the God within our fellow man as the same God within us. His message was that there was no duality whatsoever. His message was that there was only one Life, one Truth, one tree of life from which to eat. [Addington 1996, 77-80] We can abide in the Garden of Eden, Heaven within, God within, that perfect everything which is what God wants us to do, and the path is through a simply mediation on *LOVE*, the ***GOD WITHIN***. The path to enlightenment is the path of LOVE and it comes easy if we truly express LOVE within and with to ourselves and to others.

THE CENTER WITHIN - BUDDHA NATURE

"Buddhism is awareness. In our lives unless we are aware we will not see the truth, the truth about ourselves, others things and other lives." To become enlighten one must become aware of oneself. Enlightenment is beyond speech and silence. It is when we meet the morning star face to face - when we meet the God within. Beyond speech and beyond silence is the true world. "The whole world is enlighten. You are enlightened. Just open your life and meet it directly, intimately. For this you need awareness. You try to find enlightenment elsewhere, but it is here in your everyday life. The star is here, and shinning. [Kubose 1986, 1-3]

Every little thing, which we do, is the "way", the "path". The "way" is found deep inside us and yet at the same time the "way" exists out there. "outside and inside become identical". [Kubose 1986, 6] You become one with the universe. When you live in the universal Way, you see life expressing itself everywhere. Life becomes an art when its is lived in this way. Each moment in life is a form of art like a poem. "When each action is an expression of life itself there is beauty and fulfillment. This is the universal path. This is everyday life, this is enlightenment, and this is the center within. [Kubose 1986, 7]

To find ourselves we should look within to find our true nature whom we are. We will often find that al the things which we complain about, all the negative things which occur n the world are within us and they must be removed in order to find the peace which we desire. We soon learn when we look within that we have many positive traits and also many negative traits, but we should not be dismayed for this is the outer program which was project into our minds. We can clear all the negative and live with loving kindness in the world without by being like the sun which *just is.* The sun shines and everyone is happy - the sun *just is.* "Be yourself. Listen to the inner voice. Buddhism teaches us to live an authentic life which is truth itself. You must live your life. When you are the center, there is tremendous joy and creativeness." [Kubose 1986, 23]

When you find your center you, you radiate out from the center with joy, love and kindness and you are like the sun shinning upon all around you and giving love. You become a part of life and you are life. When you engage yourself with others " because you can't help but do, life can be enthusiastic, very beautiful, one with all other people." [Kubose 1986, 24]

"When we get together and do things together, all become one."
[Kubose 1986, 24] We become one and real brothers and sisters just like
the American Indians when they smoke a peace pipe together, when we
share a meal together, or when we drink tea together as is done in the
Japanese tea ceremony when everyone drinks from the same bowel. Or in
"communion in Christianity, to eat Christ's flesh, to drink Christ's blood,
means to become one with Him." [Kubose 1986, 24]

"This oneness is true not only among people but also between
people and all things." For example, a flower is a living thing, when you
see that it needs water and you give it water, you are communicating with
the flower and you have become one with the flower, you and the flower
are one. "This is true of everything else in the world. By looking within,
you become aware of and one with all things. Buddhism teaches you how
to live from the inside to the outside. Look within and live your true life."
{Kubose 1986, 24]

When you look within you find your true self, a self which you
may not like but as you look deep within you, you will find LOVE, GOD,
the GOD WITHIN. When you find this LOVE, you can radiate it out to
the entire universe and become one with the entire universe and find
GOD and LOVE in all things. In this way God's love, your love will be one
with all like the sun shinning on all. Your true self will radiate to all the·
world. You will be at peace. You will walk the path of loving kindness, the
path of GOD WITHIN, the path of Jesus, Buddha, and all the mystic
masters. It is your path - the center within and you live in the awareness
of God Within and Without and it *just is*! When you hold the thought in
your mind through out all the moments of time, *LOVE JUST IS* like the
sun radiating life to all then you are LOVE and you are one with all and
one with GOD. Your are enlighten and at peace.

On your way to enlightenment and peace it is good to live in the
"Middle Way" that is the "Middle Way is Life Itself. We live today, and
we live in this very moment." [Kubose 1986, 42] The Buddhist concept
of time is not historical. Rather, it is a series of points of moments. The
past is already gone, and the future is yet to come. The reality of time is
just the present, this very moment. Also, we should not become attached
to the mid-point because life is a continuous process because a soon as
we say this is the mid-point it is already gone. This way of looking at life
is very important for living life and awareness because we are living now,
not in the past or the future. [Kubose 1986, 42-43] It is important to live
now and being aware — this is meditation in the now - full awareness in
everything and "oneness and no mind".

No only do we share a oneness in time, but a oneness in life.
"The essence of life is one." When we realizes this oneness of life, we

becomes peaceful. We do not fight against conditions but are free to become one with such conditions. In the same way that water changes it shape according to the shape that it is in. Water adapts itself according to the conditions that it is in and at the same time water remain water and never changes its essential nature. In the same way our minds should be like water that is flexible and yet maintaining our essential nature and awareness. Our mind should be like a great ocean accepting all things and yet be not upset by them. "There are no tensions or complexes of any kind in the great-ocean mind. Water is Buddhistic; we can see many teachings in the nature of water." Kubose 1986, 45-46]

"In Buddhism 'no mind' means that in living life you should not have a mind that controls you. 'No mind' means to be yourself, just as you are - natural, with no self-conscious, purpose - with no explanation. No mind means, 'Just is'." [Kubose 1986, 50]. No mind is like water. "Water has no intention of flowing. It does not say, 'I have to flow this way; I have to flow that way.'" [Kubose 1986, 50] The life of no mind it the flowing of life from within, that is life must flow out from within. It is the doing which bring satisfaction to life, awareness, peace, love and mediation in the moment. In the similar fashion of children at play. They put their total life into playing. Mediation in the moment is play, no mind, the doing and flowing like water with the oneness of life.

Oneness and no mind helps to understand that "Every day is a good day". The day itself is good but when we make comparison according to our expectations we can made the day bad. However, we must focus our minds to realize that every day is a good day. "To understand that ever day is a good day is Buddhism. This is the content of enlightenment. Enlightenment is not something apart from ordinary day. Enlightenment is to live each day as a good day." [Kubose 1986, 88-89] Enlightenment is finding your center within from which all of life flows. "Life becomes meaningful and all life opens up for you." [Kubose 1986, 111]

Meaningful life comes to you through meditation, which means serenity in life. "Many people think that meditation is to sit cross- legged. That is only a small part of meditation. Nor is just being quiet necessarily serenity. True serenity is dynamic like a generator revolving at the speed of thousands of revolution per minute - very stable, very quiet, but very dynamic." [Kubose 1986, 114] Serenity of meditation is a strength which comes deep from within. When express as quietness it is deep and serene and as action it is dynamic and harmonious. We can maintain this serenity by centering our lives, which enables to see the "truth of life". "Our minds, when we are serene, are able to reflect the truth about life and all things." This is what we call meditation. [Kubose 1986, 114 - 115]

The truth about life is that all things change, things are not always the same which is the basic teaching of Buddhism. Life is constant change. Our ego fears change, consequently we must be ego-less, and most of all are egos do not want to die. "However, when we are born it has. already been decided that we will die. Birth and death are not two things. Death is included in life. Life means death. Without death there is no birth. The world is beautiful because it changes. Once we realize that all stage of change are beautiful, then we realize the reality of one-ness which is that all stage are beautiful only once. This is *mu jo.* If we understand, this we are able to take whatever comes and live life to it's fullest. That is to live in the moment and in peace. For "peace is when things change naturally. Water flows peacefully. Fire burns peacefully. Life moves peacefully. Peace is not stable or constant. Peace is dynamic. Peace of mind is to know things as they are. If you live in *mu jo,* life is beautiful. Every moment is precious. This the basic Buddhist teaching of impermanence or continuous change." [Kubose 1986, 116-118]   If we accept change as beautiful, our lives become a meditation of continues peace, change and beauty and all the moments are full of beauty, *LOVE* and *PEACE, and death becomes birth and birth becomes death and we become one with God and Love, Peace and Beauty is always with us for God is with us and within us.*

To find the center within, we must transcend a means-end kind of thinking. We must go beyond the attitude for being motivated to act only in order to get something. "True realty is only when seeker and sought are one. The very doing is the realization of the Buddha's way. When you wash dishes, wash dishes - nothing else. When you sleep, you sleep - nothing else. When you do something put your whole life into it." [Kubose 1986, 119] We should "not seek things. The means is the end in itself. To transcend duality is the Buddha Dharama itself. The more you realize this the deeper you will understand the reality of life in all things. This is the Buddhist teaching of transcending means and ends. [Kubose 1986, 119] The very doing is a living mediation which we can do in every moment which centers us and makes us one with the God within resulting in the lost of all duality and become one with the universal God conscious. This helps us to have the right understanding that the most important thing is here and now, how you live in the present moment. We should "live each day most beautifully and most meaningfully. This is important because all things are subject to change. Life is transitory; we should live each day the best we can. Then if anything happens there is not regret. Each day is complete in itself. Live every day sincerely because each day is the last day". [Kubose 1986, 125] The Buddha's teaching, "Ichigo, ichie" means "one life, meets only once" This means that we only meet once in a life time. [Kubose 1986, 124] We meet one moment only once in a lifetime. Consequently, our living meditation is to live in that moment with are complete focus and no duality and to experience the beauty and meaning of life in moment which creates LOVE, PEACE and ONE-NESS with GOD.

As we move forward with our journey to enlightenment, we find ·that there are many paths to ONE-NESS with GOD. One of the most interesting paths is that of the Kundalini and the chakras, the spiritual path of India. We shall begin our journey in this path Edgar Cayce, 'the sleeping prophet'.

THE BOOK OF REVELATIONS:
THE BIBLICAL THEORY OF THE CHAKRAS

According to the according the ancient spiritual traditions of the India, the working of the Kundalini energy through the openings of the chakras WAS A HIGHLY VALUED AND GUARDED SECRET. This energy is the key to the fountain of youth, the power of rejuvenation, the creative energy found in the human body. [Reed 1988, 185] It is here that the Creator [God] meets man and they become ONE.

Edgar Cayce while in a psychic trance stated that the Book of Revelations written by the Apostle John is a record of John's experience of cosmic consciousness - a Kundalini awakening which john experience within in his own body. During this experience the Christ Consciousness instructed John as to the meaning of the experience and asked him to take responsibility for the knowledge revealed. "The imagery in" the Book of Revelations "is a detailed account of what happens when psychic centers are opened and what must be done in order to maintain mastery over the spiritual body." [Reed 1988, 186] The psychic centers or energy centers are identified by Cayce as the endocrine system as the "body" of the super-conscious mind.

The number seven appears several times. This number corresponds to the seven glands of the endocrine systems and the seven psychic centers, or chakras. The seven "churches" are the glands, while the seven "seals" are the chakras yet to be opened. The following chart provides a diagram of the corresponds between the individual glands, the psychic centers, and the symbology in Revelation.

THE SYMBOLOGY OF THE PSYCHIC CENTERS

CHAKRA	ENDOCRINE GLAND	CHURCH IN REVELATION	PHRASES FROM THE LORD'S PRAYER
1] Root	Gonads	Ephesus	"Give us this day, our daily bread ..."
2] Water	Cells of Leydig	Smyrna	"Lead us not into temptation ..."
3] Solar Plexus	Adrenals	Pergamous	"Forgive us our debts ..."
4] Heart	Thymus	Thyatria	"In earth as it is in heaven ..."
5] Throat	Thyroid	Sardis	"Thy kingdom come; Thy will be done ..."
6] Third Eye	Pineal	Philadelphia	"Hallowed be Thy name ..." " And the power ..."
7] Crown	Pituitary	Laodicea	"Our Father, who art in heaven ..." "And the glory forever ..."

[Reed 1988, 186]

Jesus in the gospel according to Matthew gave the people a prayer, the Lord's prayer. Edgar Cayce in his psychic trance revealed that the Lord's payer is a patterning of the opening of the seven psychic centers and the circulation of those energies trough the body. Similar to the Eastern traditions, the opening of the energies involves a pattern which places the higher centers in charge of the opening of the entire systems. This is the awakening of the Kundalini energy as shown in the forgoing chart.

When we say "Our Father Who art in Heaven", the energy begins flowing in the crown chakra because the pituitary is the master gland influencing all others. This energy flowing from the super-conscious mind - the God mine - begins the activation of all the other chakras. As we say "Hallowed be thy Name" the prayer, the spirit of God, the White Light, proceeds down through the pineal gland and to the thyroid or the will center with the saying of "They kingdom come; they will be done" which involves the sacrifice or "death" of the individual, the separatist will of the conscious mind. With the saying of "On earth as it is in Heaven" harmony in action is created with the upper and lower centers, with the super-conscious with the conscious, with the heart center [thymus]. This is the center which is the inter-mediating center between the upper and lower centers. From this point the prayer moves done to the root chakra when we say "Give us this day our daily bread" and the shift focus to calm the adrenals upon saying "Forgive us our debts" by removing fear and anxiety. Saying of "Lead us not into temptation" brings us into a relationship with the cells of Leydig which influence creativity enabling us not to squander creative energy. Then, this creative energy begins it path upward to the higher centers beginning with the heart center when we say "Deliver us from evil", and continuing up culminating at the crown chakra. We can repeat the cycle, again and again, as the energy circulates, transforming us more and more to become one with God by transforming the cells in the body. The overall theme of the prayer is to put the energies into the services of the super-conscious mind. "The prayer is focused on serene state of mind based upon voluntary surrender to a higher power." [Reed 1988, 188-189] In this way the Lord's Prayer teaches us to become one with the Christ Conscious, with God, with Jesus, with the Father, with the Spirit, with the God Within and the God Without and we become a Channel for the Holy Spirit and in this way we open the KUNDALINI and open the Third Eye.

ON THE JOURNEY TO THE KINGDOM OF GOD -
THE TRUE SECRET OF MEDITATION

When we open the third eye and awaken the Kundalini, we are on the path of finding the True Spirit [God] the Wisdom Mind. On this journey to the Kingdom of God within, the feet and hand of the mind meet every possible barrier. However, we can break through these barriers by following the paths of the Ancient Wisdom and the Mystery Schools of Egypt and India. The opening of the third eye and the Kundalini can be accomplished through what the prophet and saints in *The Bible* refer to as the Sound Current, they often call it **THE WORD**. The Mystery Schools of Antiquity referred to it as The Lost Word or the Lost Chord — "implying that man at one time had possession of The Word or the Divine Sound Current and through his journey into the realms of matter, lost contact with it. The Vedas- the holy writings of ancient seers and rishis of India — called it the Holy Nad. The saints of Islam call it Kalma. Moslem Sufis of today call it the Holy Shabd. [Chaney 1980, 12]

The sound current is "the out-breathing of the Divine Word issuing from the Creator, a Cosmic Sound through which all the worlds came into being, and which man himself is caused to live and have his being. The Sound Current is the Holy Ghost of the Bible." [Chaney 1980, 46] The great masters of the Mystery Schools of Ancient Egypt executed their magical rituals through the use of Words of Power. Those who could use the Words of Power to the fullest were known as the Sons of Light. Even in those days of antiquity the Symbol and the Word *AUM* or *OM* omnificent power - a Word containing a concentrated storehouse of force, at once dynamic and intelligence. "It is *AUM* and its mysterious symbolism which has become the Lost Word initiates and mystics have sought for the ages, ever since its true meaning faded into the mists of time. In ancient Egypt the letters *A-U-M* came to represent the three powers combined in the Trinity of the Deity." [Chaney 1980, 54] The sound *AUM* contains the secret divine name. It is an imperishable Word according to the Upanishad [the Holy Book of the Hindu's]. It is the past, present and future. All that was, and is and will be is *AUM*. [Chaney 1980, 54].

A-U-M is at once an invocation and a benediction. In the Mystery Schools, AUM was always used as the affirmative salutary prayer to the Deity. It was again used as the closing affirmation. Spoken in the beginning, it open man's being to the down pouring of flow of Divine energies contained in the scared Words. Spoken at the close of the affirmation as a benediction, it sealed the aura so as to hold the being as a closed chalice through which the Divine energies might response and bring birth the Christ within as the embryo floated in the Divine Elixir or waters of the AUM. The word Amen used to terminate a prayer is a modern rendition of the ancient Aum. [Chaney 1980, 56]

Used as a mantric sound, AUM or OM becomes the energy which links us with GOD. It stirs the chakric force centers within and stimulates and awakens God Within, the Kundalini force making the journey up to unite with GOD without. This causes us to become one with the universe the Cosmic Divinity, with GOD within and without. When we use this wonderful power of sound, we also should use this power of sound with visualization and breathing to open the THIRD EYE [the Brow Chakra, also known as the Wisdom Eye].

To absorb the highest power from a mantra, it should be combine with breath. That is mentally chanting the mantra when inhaling and again while exhaling. With each inhalation, prana stirs the inner being, merging with the power of the mantra. The technique of visualizing the flowing prana merging with the power of the sound — aligns the physical body with the more subtle bodies: the astral, mental, causal, and celestial bodies:

1] Inhale, chanting the mantra, visualizing prana, and directing the flow down the spine to the root chakra. 2] Exhale and chant, seeing the prana flowing up again to the third eye.

This practice becomes spontaneous pranayama or breath control. At the same time, it purifies the physical form with pranic flow throughout the cells and blood stream. Bio-magnetism flows upward, flooding the aura with White Light, drawing down the grace of the Oversoul. [Chaney 1980, 50]

This sound of the sacred word *AUM* or *OM* is the *I AM* of the Lord Jesus that which existed BEFORE ABRAHAM came into human existence, that is the Great Cosmic, the Spirit of God, [Chaney 1980, 57] that is God. When we repeatedly say the word *AUM [I AM],* we experience the journey of becoming one with *GOD* and the White Light of God flows through us releasing us into the energy of GOD and we are with GOD, both within and without [the Cosmic Universe *of GOD*] and experience divine illumination, the wisdom mind of *GOD.*

When we combine breathing, with chanting the word AUM and looking into the glowing flame of a candle we begin to visualize the inner flame which stimulate the pituitary and pineal glands which opens the Third Eye since the flame of the candle is slowly transferred as a Divine Light in the Center of the brain.

"Eventually you will merge your entire being into this inner light as the consciousness draws inward, inward, inward, and, from the center of the Third Eye, begins to flow upward, opening the Crown chakra to receive the down-pouring grace" [Chaney 1980, 70] from God. You can end this meditation of the inner light by lying flat in the energy field and see yourself with the in-flowing stream of WHITE LIGHT and know that every atom, cell, gland and muscle is being transformed. You may even experience and out of body journey into inner space. Also, this is a good time to say an affirmation of your choice for example

> **I am surrounded by the Pure White Light of the Christ, Nothing but good can come to me. Nothing but good shall go from me. I give thanks. I give thanks. I give thanks. [Chaney 1980, 70]**

After this affirmation, it is now possible to return to *THIS* world of physical reality and you are ready to perform your Dharmic duties of everyday life, but you are one with GOD and now ready to experience the "Effortless Effort" like the ZEN Buddhist who floats effortlessly on the river of time and allows the river to carry him. [Chaney 1980, 76] You become totally aware and one with GOD in all things. This is the true secret of meditation.

THE ACCESSION INTO THE LIGHT - THE GOD WITHOUT

When Jesus left this world, his soul asented into GOD into the light [energy] into the God without. We can all make this same journey as the Great Master Jesus and it does not require many hours of meditation. Rather, it requires a mind set and visualization. First, we are going to ascent into the Celestial Sanctum which is the highest plane of consciousness where one may receive the blessings of the ***Cosmic - GOD!*** Please proceed in the following manner:

1] Wash your hands as symbol of bodily purification, dry them well and drink a glass of water to symbolize your desire for purity on the inter plane.

2] Sit in a relax position in a quiet place, close your eyes and recite the following invocation mentally:

> **May the Divine Essence of the Cosmic infuse my being and cleanse me of all impurities of mind and body, that I may enter the Celestial Sanctum and attune in pureness and worthiness. So mote It Be! [AMORC 1994, 7]**

The goal of this invocation is to express a desire to the Cosmic [God] for attainment of the Celestial Sanctum in consciousness and to communicate with the wisdom that it symbolizes on the mystical plane.

3] After reciting this invocation, take deep breaths and fully relax. In hale deeply through the noise in a regular and rhythmic way. Once you are fully relax, breathe normally and ***begin to imagine that you are ASCENDING TO YOUR CELESTIAL SANCTUM.*** Visualize you are ascending the room where you are, you are ascending your home, town, and Earth. Then, slowly turn your gaze towards the infinite cosmic continuing your spiritual ascent until you perceive the Celestial Sanctum you have visualized. The fact, you can see your Celestial Sanctum rising in the Cosmic and bathing in the celestial light, should fill you with an indescribable inner joy. As you enter your Celestial Sanctum which can be whatever you want it to be for example a temple, landscape, the light of GOD, become one with it and unaware of the earthly plane and live completely at the level of the soul. "All your thoughts and emotions will be impressed with great serenity and well-being that no physical satisfaction can bring about." [AMORC 1994, 8] Upon entering the celestial sanctum, "let yourself be totally immersed in the scared, inspiring, and comforting feelings which pervade it. With body and soul bating in this atmosphere, the time has arrived for you to express, to the God of your heart the reason for your coming to this place of high spiritually." [AMORC 1994, 8] After presenting the reason which made you ascend to the celestial Sanctum and when you place yourself in a state of total receptivity, you will receive a cosmic influx that will answer you question, for example cure you, inspire you, bring the answer which you are seeking. At the end of the period of receptivity, gradually return to the objective plane. See yourself leaving your Celestial Sanctum and returning to your home. Upon return to the objective consciousness, open your eyes and say the following invocation:

> **May the God of my Heart sanctify this at-attunement of self with the Celestial Sanctum! So Mote It Be!** [AMORC 1994, 9]

The Celestial Sanctum is not a place, rather a field of cosmic energy, a level of high spirituality, an exalted plane of consciousness which completely transcends time and place. Consequently, no matter where you are you may enter the Celestial Sanctum. You do not have to have a problem or a question prior to enter the Celestial Sanctum. You can enter it for the sheer inner satisfaction it provides. " In this case, the Cosmic bestows the blessings it deems wise to give to us. In fact, we can have at least one reason for wanting to reach this particular state of consciousness, and that *is to pray for the happiness of others and for Peace on earth.* " [AMORC 1994, 10]

YOU ARE A SOUL THAT HAS A BODY —
. GOING WITHOUT AND BLENDING WITH ENERGY, LIGHT AND THE UNIVERSE [GOD WITHOUT]

The *soul* is the creative part of you, the uniqueness which recognizes yourself as an individual. It is your identity, it is above and beyond the physical structure of the brain. The *soul* is not necessarily a religious term, rather it is the complete, conscious, creative you, a unique consciousness, the essence of your humanity. [Sanders 1989, 196]

Peter J. Sanders, Jr. [1989, 196 - 206] states he can teach us a method for taping our Soul energy which is a pathway by which we can extend our soul into matter, light and the far corners of the universe, to use the soul to access heightened consciousness and increase creativity, and most important to cross the portal of the Soul to reach unlimitedness. When you learn to tape your soul you are at the gateway of unlimited potential. Through it you enter a realm of infinitely flexible energy. You are energy! Einstein's $E = mc2$ equation states that energy equals mass times the speed of light square. That is all things are energy, only they appear in different forms. The chair is energy. Light is energy. You are energy!

"The law of conservation of energy states, *energy can be neither created or destroyed, only changed in form*. That means that you, as energy are now, always have been and always will be. The only questions is to what you will do with your energy. Will you limit and suppress it? Or will your reach for your unlimitedness?" [Sanders 1989, 206] You can prove the unlimitedness of your Soul energy by expanding beyond the awareness of the physical boundaries of your body. When you realize you are a soul with a body, you no longer limit yourself to physical capabilities. You have the ability to blend and be one with all things. [Sanders 1989, 206]

Sanders [1989, 198] states that most of the energy which exists as you as the Soul exists outside the body that is above the head and slightly behind it with part of it extending down into the head area linking the brain and physical sense and coordinates the machinery of the body. The soul energy is located around the head which is the reason people can see an aura around the head and paintings of saints and major religious figures always portray the halo there.

With the development of the Super String Theory, science and spirituality took a giant leap to close the gap between them. This theory explains the mathematically the structure and relationship of all forces and particles which exist in the cosmos, from the smallest subatomic particles to gravity and nuclear attraction.

> **What connects Super-string Theory to the exploration of consciousness and the Soul is the fact that its mathematical foundations requires the existence of ten dimensions. Physicists are coming to accept that all things - a chair, a lion, a planet, even you - exists in ten dimensions rather than the four which we are familiar with [the three spatial dimensions of height, breadth and length, plus the fourth dimension of time]. the other six dimensions are still beyond our ability to identify, much less to measure with current technology.**
>
> **The concept of other dimensions is not new. Astronomers and astrophysicist have long proposed that material being sucked into black holes may actually be compressed and shot through an extra-dimensional back door to distant portions of the universe - or even other universes - where it emerges from white holes. The key point is that the Super-string Theory applies extra-dimensionality to *all of us*, not just to back holes or science fiction stories. Perhaps, the unique consciousness that is you — the Soul — exists in some of those added dimensions. [Sanders 1989, 197]**

We all are souls. We "may think of the Soul as being that unique energy pattern or field that lies beyond the transience of physical matter, and outside the limited forms of currently measurable energy. In terms of the Super-string Theory, it would be those additional six dimensions we all have." To tap your full potential, you must realize you are a soul that has a body and not limited by your body. [Sanders 1989, 204 - 205]

We can shift our Soul into these other dimensions by focusing our awareness up and out to the more extensive portion of Soul energy above the head. The key is to focus that is to selectively heighten your awareness among the inner direction which your are exploring, allowing it to flow along the path of your search. To experience your Soul, learn to focus your awareness gently, like an inner form of peripheral vision during your meditations. Tapping the Soul even briefly relieves the pressure of the physical world. In most instances one's aura will unwind and expand two to six inches by the time your meditation is over. "Once your learn your control, the soul-shift can be used throughout your day. You can blend into any object and sense it as an extension of yourself. You can gradually become a part of more and more around you." [Sanders 1989, 201- 206]

You can blend yourself into the universe within and without by using the following meditation:

> **Gently float and enjoy the feeling of You, your Soul Nature. After a short while, allow that awareness to expand so that it gradually includes your whole being. Feel the real You become one with your physical body. Feel your body melt and blend into your awareness of yourself. At this point, you may be experiencing for the first time the complete fullness of your total self — body, mind, and Soul. You should feel like one big ball of awareness, extending beyond the limits of your body paradoxically penetrating deeper into the fabric of your physical being than you normally experience [Sanders 1989, 207]**

and expanding outward to blend with the energy and light of the universe, with GOD.

The next step is to experience walking in oneness with all things without meditation and your eyes open. That is sensing in and above the plane of the physical world at the same time. This known as bi-level awareness which is a quantum leap in consciousness. With bi-level awareness, you no longer need to close your eyes or meditate to reach a higher consciousness and deeper Soul skills. This awareness can be achieved by focusing and blending your awareness with all things around you. [Sanders 1989, 225] and becoming one with God within and without — a blending of the within with the without.

Now, we have completed our journey to become with God within and without. We have discussed various methods for obtaining one with GOD, and we have become one with God in writing and contemplating the aforesaid and we hope that have accomplished the same for the reader of the aforesaid. My you go in peace and with GOD - Amen [AUM] and so it is!

CHAPTER IV
DISCUSSION

When we enter the earth dimension for whatever reason, we realize that we are on a journey to reunite with the Supreme Being - God within and without, god all around us and in us. As children until the age of three or four, we are very much with God, there is almost no separation from us and the God within and without. However, as we become older we .receive all the projections or energies of others into our energy field, into our soul, into our spirit, and we lose GOD. We become inundated with fear, anger, greed, hate, — pain and suffering of all forms resulting from attachments. We lose are relationship with the Supreme Being and we are along in fighting a war against the bombardment of the ungodly energies invading us from all directions.

Some of us become crazy, most of us cannot cope, we are in deep pain, so much pain that we want to find God again as soon as possible, but the road to God is forgotten and we have to relearn the path to God.

The Christian Bible is one path to God if one understand the deep metaphysical meaning of this Bible. By reading and understanding the Bible in a metaphysical way one can gain God again, one can obtain a high spiritual path and walk with the Supreme Being. One can know God again and be with God. This BOOK can be used as a map to walking in a Godly path and being one with God. This BOOK can make you one with God by mediating on the deeper metaphysical meanings of the Bible whose words of love can being you inner peace and God.

Also, there is another path to God, this is the water way, the way of the Buddhist who go with the flow of life and live every moment of life as if it were the last moment. The living in the moment with no past or future, the clam of being with God in everything that one does during every moment of one's life. This is the practical way of being in the now and excepting the flow of God within you and around you and living as though one knew there was only one beautiful moment in time that continues for ever more. This is the beauty of knowing that God *just is* and living in the nothingness of the now. This path brings inner peace because it *just is* and God is just in you and flows with you in all things. This path creates great mental calmness and love. This path creates a balance and serene mind and excellent mental health.

Another method of finding your way back to God, the Supreme Being is to awaken you chakras or energy field within your body. There are various methods for awaken the Christ energy or Kundalini energy within you. Edgar Cayce suggest that repeating the Christian Lords prayer is method for waking the Kundalini energy or god energy within us. By circulating this energy through our bodies may times, we awaking the God within us and we realize we are one with God. This creates a wonderful knowing in us and returns us to God. Thus, creating harmony and balance within and without us, creating love and peace for us and raising the conscious of are spirit to being one with God again.

Another method for awaking God within us is atone our bodies and minds to the sound of God or the Word of God which is the sound of AUM or I AM. If we make our bodies vibrate with this sound we open up our third eye and the wisdom of God enters our being and we are one with God. We return to the God being within us which we were born with but lost as a child.

Additionally, we can find God and speak to God by ascending to our Celestial Sanctum. This is ascending to the place of the flow with the interaction with the Cosmic GOD without which is also the Universal God within. You create a sanctum for yourself where you meet with God and communicate with God, God speaks to you and you speak to God. This is a field of cosmic energy, a level of high spiritually were you communicate to the Supreme Being on a one to one bases and where you can receive guidance from God. Speaking to God gives one a great sense of calmness and balance because now you know that you are in direct communication with the Supreme Being of love and kindness and you life in the earth dimension will be one of love and kindness.

Finally, when you open your mind and heart and you realize that you are a part of the energy which is the God, you *blend with that energy in all things* and you reach the Unlimitedness of God. You are energy which can be neither created nor destroyed which means that you are now, always have been and always will be. You live in the peace, joy, love and calmness of knowing you are one with God.

If those engaging in professional metaphysics would assist others in become one with God that is as many as they can for example through mass communication and training programs, then many individuals would have an opportunity to live in the beauty and calmness of being one with God and this would raise the conscious of humanity to high levels of love and peace. This is the purpose of the information contained in the aforesaid and should be the goal of all of mankind.

CHAPTER V
SUMMARY AND CONCLUSION

This study is story of finding one's path to God. There are many paths to finding God within and without, and just God in everything. Sometimes and perhaps most of the time it become very hard to be one with God or the Supreme Being or whatever you may call the Energy. It is very hard because our minds are quickly filled up with the bombardment of energies from numerous sources, none of which see to be very Godly. We struggle with pain and suffering because we have lost our way, and often times practice avoiding the way to God because we fool ourselves into thinking and believing the path to God is to hard. We do not realize that the way to God is to find the center within and without. Once we are in the center, we are in the void, the calmness of nothing-ness, and the energy of no energy the spirit of GOD. We are there within and without God, we are God and God is us.

We simply could find God by drawing a circle, a medicine wheel, place a point the center of the circle look into the point in the center and there is God, and there we are in our relationship with God and ourselves. We are centered and with God. However, for most this is too easy, and other more elaborate means or paths or methodologies are used to find God, and much more time and effort. In the aforesaid study, some of these paths have been offered as a means of helping our souls find God again. These paths may work for some of you and not for others, or you may have your own path for finding God while in the earth dimension, and perhaps you may find God at all until your body prepares to died and your soul and spirit leave your earth body and re-unites with God. No matter what happens, you will eventually re-unite with God. For some, it is better to have this union with God as soon as possible while occupying the human body of the earth dimension because they have calling to find God in this very moment. For others, it is of no concern in that they are not in search of God. There is no wrong way or right way or moment in time when you find God. There is only your way and God's way which only God and you know. This is your way and may God always be with you. Amen!

BOOK 2
CHAPTER 1
INTRODUCTION

Our purpose is to understand the use of *MIRACLES* to heal the body, mind, soul and spirit. A *MIRACLE* "is something which cannot happen by human means" [Cerullo 1995, 3]. That is "a miracle is a supernatural manifestation of God that comes into our daily lives to deal with events and circumstances that cannot be met by just the normal means" [Cerullo, 1995, 4]. As we progress through life, at times we call upon God to assist us out of our problems which often cause great mental and physical pain. We seek help from all sorts of healers from modern .western medicine to shamans. We want the pain removed in order that we may function pain free and follow our earth path to its fullest. In seeking the removal of pain, often times we do not want to deal with the spiritual or have no knowledge of how to deal with the spiritual. Even through the causes of disease may be infection, environmental toxicities or nutritional deficiencies, the reason why people come down with these diseases are spiritual, and even if the treatments are physical, the reason why people heal are also spiritual. Perhaps the highest Universal Medicine is the Buddha Nature which is God, the Christ Consciousness, the Highest Self. [Forshang Buddhism, 63]

God is a God of miracles who is the same everyday. God is a supernatural God who is the same yesterday, today, and forever [Hebrews 13:8]. Men change, churches change structure. Theology changes but God never changes - for God has no beginning or end [Cerullo 1995, 6]. For the Greatest Miracle is not physical but spiritual [Hinn 1994, 1]. Perhaps, the Greatest Miracle is the use of energy that comes to us direct from God and comes to us to produces *MIRACLES* that remove pain from the spirit, the soul, the mind, and the body while we are partaking in our earth walk. This *MIRACLE OF ENERGY* that comes directly from God can be accessed by all of us and can be used to create miracles for ourselves and others

God is *ENERGY*! God is sound and light! God is spirit! God is *MIRACLES!* Ancient alchemist and primitive shamans knew that every physical form is a unique pattern, developed by electric energy which permeates the atmosphere. However, quantum physicists only recently discovered that if matter is broken down into smaller and smaller pieces [electron, protons, etc.], it eventually reaches a point when it is no longer an object but a wave of energy. When matter is broken down again and again, it has no dimensions cannot be measured. [Talbot 1991, 33].

What this means is that the "world in which we live is no longer static when our thoughts, perceptions, and impressions are in synchronistic harmony with the cosmic rhythms of Nature and the Earth" [Elsbeth 1997, 51] and God. The universe is made of energy waves of rhythms of Nature, Earth, Spirit, and God. There is evidence the only time energy waves become matter is when we are looking at them. When we are not looking at them, they remain as waves of energy. [Talbot 1991, 33]. This "finding reiterates what shamans and alchemists have know all along: *only conscious perception alters reality as we know it* . The Earth is a vast sea of vibrating energy. Everything vibrates to the rhythm of the COSMOS" [Elsbeth 1997, 52] - GOD.

This study is a manual for creating miracles that remove pain and suffering and which can makes us all healers through the use of the God Energy. These forms of energy have been known through out the ages by different names but they are all derived from God. The *GOD ENERGIES* which we will learn to use and create miracles are: 1] Charismatic Healing - Word of God and Prayer, 2] Pranic Healing, 3] Reiki Healing, and 4] Radiatory Healing - Biomagnetism. These *ENERGIES or SPIRITS* which are both positive and negative *[THE SHADOW SPIRITS]* and flow from the COSMOS shall be studied in this paper as a means of learning how to use these energies to heal the
body, mind, soul and spirit.

CHAPTER II

CHARISMATIC HEALING
THE WORD OF GOD AND PRAYER

GOD IS A GOD OF MIRACLES: *God* is always there for you. There are many reasons why people have not experience miracles. However, the biggest reasons is that man is self limited by the environment which he creates for himself, that is his own personal environment. If you live in expectations of miracles, God can and will supernaturally provide them. If necessary God will send an angel [spirit] or use someone else to give you the miracle which you need. Miracles are the natural characteristic of God. People look at miracles as the exception, but God is trying to teach us that miracles should be the normal experience of our lives, because God's character is to perform miracles. He does not do anything to the contrary to His Nature. Therefore, miracles are not unnatural. They are a natural flow of God's Love for us! [Cerullo 1995, 2-5]

Miracles can be created if you follow the following steps: 1] See God as God is. 2] Take your eyes off your circumstances. 3] See your problem as a miracle opportunities. 4] Realize in every promise of God is the seed for your miracle. 5] Plant a miracle seed ... act on God's Word. Then claim God's miracle provisions: 1] Salvation, 2] Healing, 3] Deliverance, 4] Prosperity, 5] Guidance, 5] Strength, and 7] Peace. [Cerullo 1995, 166- 169].

In order for a miracle to happen, we must see GOD as GOD is. For "all things are possible with God" [The Bible, Mark 10:27]. You must see God as God is that is ... all powerful, all knowing, everywhere present. Men have failed to recognize God. They have failed to see God as their Deliverer, their Provider, and their Healer. Most people who believe there is a God, do not know him as their heavenly Father Who loves and cares ·for them as a natural father cares for his children. [The Bible, Luke 12:6-7] Most people also do not realize that God is waiting to help anyone who calls upon God. For the eyes of the Lord run to and fro throughout the whole earth, to show God as strong on the behalf of those whose heart is loyal to God [The Bible, Chronicles 16:9].

Charismatic believe that the only way to see God is through *JESUS - THE CHRIST.* There is only way that man can have God revealed to him. Man cannot know and see God through his own intellect. It is impossible. The natural mind is incapable of comprehending God's greatness. God has made this clear in God's word [Cerullo 1995, 25]: "but the natural receiveth not the things of the Spirit of God: for they are foolishness unto him: neither can he know them, because they are spiritually discerned" [The Bible, 1 Corinthians 2:14]. Neither can man reach God through his good works [The Bible, Ephesians 2:8-9]. "If he tries any other way than what God has directed, he is only fooling himself "[Cerullo 1995, 25]. Jesus said, "I am the way, the truth, and the life: no man cometh unto the Father, but by me:" [The Bible, John 14:6]. Therefore, the only way in which we can see God as he is, is through Jesus the Christ. When an individual accepts Christ into his or her life, the greatest miracle happens. They are born again, and become a new person with new desires and a new spiritual mind [The Bible, 1 Corinthians 5:17]. The spirit of God is supernatural implanted within [The Bible, Romans 8:8-9], and through the Spirit it is possible to see God and to know the miracle provisions GOD has made for us [The Bible, Ephesians 1:17-18].

FAITH: After you see God as God, you must have *FAITH* ! With the acceptance of Jesus comes faith. For by grace you are saved through faith and that not of yourselves, it is the gift of God [The Bible, Ephesians 2:8-9]. Use the faith that God has given you. Release the faith which God has given you and believe in God to supernaturally intervene to give you miracles. God will heal you if you have faith in God to do so. Also, if you do not have faith, God can and does work through the faith of someone else. To see God and receive God's miracle provisions for your life, you must come to God in and through the gift of faith God has given you. You must believe that *GOD IS*, and God is a rewarder of those who diligently seek God [The Bible, Hebrews 11:6, James 1:6]. You do not need to struggle for faith to reach God. As you receive Christ into your life you receive faith as a gift [The Bible, Ephesians 2:8]. These two basic truths, your acceptance of Jesus the Christ and God's gift of faith, are the foundations for miracles. [Cerullo 1995, 23 -29]

SEE GOD AS GOD IS: If you are going to be successful with God, you must have a clear understanding of God and realize that God is not limited by time or space. God has the ability to be everywhere-present all at one time. God is a Spirit that exist everywhere in the universe, in the cosmos. God is the Supreme Being which means the highest in rank and authority of all beings. God is supernatural, unlimited, unchanging, ever present and ever willing to meet our needs. God is relevant to us at the point of our need. There is not a situation, a problem, a need which we face that is impossible with God. We must take very limitation of time and space and cast it aside. Throw out any and all preconceived ideas how we desire God to meet our needs. Deal with God as God is, not as we are, and we shall be one step closer to a miracle. [Cerullo 1995, 29-37]

TAKE YOUR EYES OFF YOUR CIRCUMSTANCES: Miracles occur when you take your eyes off the circumstances. The moment tragedy strikes, people are paralyzed by fear. They act on impulse, panic! After the initial shock of what has happened subsides, to alleviate the pain and pressure of the moment, we try to place blame on someone else or upon God. " Oh God, why did You allow this to happen to me? Don't You care about me any more? This burden is too hard to bear. Why me, God?" [Cerullo 1995, 39]

There are two forces behind your circumstances, that is the negative, evil or Satan who wants to use your circumstances to defeat you and accuse God, and God wants to intervene in your circumstance to meet you at the point of your need and give a miracle. Some people make a big mistake by not acknowledging the existence of evil forces affecting their circumstances. They do not acknowledge the enemy of their soul — Satan. Satan is real. In God's Word he is called the destroyer because his purpose is to destroy [The Bible, Revelation 9:11]. Satan is not confine to hell but is walking through the earth and his purpose is to kill, steal and destroy [The Bible, 1 Peter 5:8]. We are dealing with spiritual warfare. This is the warfare against principalities, against powers, against rulers of the darkness of this world, against spiritual wickedness in high places [The Bible, Ephesians 6:12]. "Satan is defeated and has no power over you except what you allow him to have. You are actually carrying on spiritual warfare with an enemy who has already been defeated" [Cerullo 1995, 49].

As you take your second step towards your miracle by taking your eyes off the circumstance, you must also be able to deal with the *negative forces of unbelief*. The moment you begin to see God as God is you and believe in miracles, you will have to deal with those who are the forces of negative unbelief. You will be made fun of and criticized! When you refuse to listen to negative forces that surround you and keep your eyes on God and God's abilities, *your prayers will be answered*. "God will proved manna from heaven to keep His promised word. When others think you are foolish and try to discourage you from stepping out in faith to believe god for a miracle ... turn your back on their unbelief, take your eyes off your circumstances and keep right on walking. each step will be a miracle." [Cerullo 1995, 53 & 55].

SEE YOU PROBLEMS AS A MIRACLE OPPORTUNITIES: Once you understand that God wants to us your circumstances for your good regardless of how difficult or trying they are, you will have peace of mind and a foolproof way for you to be able to face every circumstance in your life without being overcome by fear! [Cerullo 1995, 57] God wants you to be free from fear, worry and anxiety. He wants you to cast all your cares upon him [The Bible, 1 Peter 5:7]. God wants you to develop trust in GOD ... Trust in the Lord with all thine heart; and lean not unto thine own understanding. In all the ways acknowledge God, and God shall direct your path [The Bible, Proverbs 3:5-6].

God wants you to react to your problems with faith and trust in God not pain, sorrow, rejection, anger, resentment, worry, and/or loneliness. Many people try to release these emotions churning inside them by crying bitter tears, taking long walks, searching for a quiet place to sort things out and/or looking for comfort in a friend. People often submerge themselves in these negative emotions without recognizing it. They spend hours going over and over a problem in their minds. They cannot think of anything else. Worry so clouds their minds it not only affects their thinking and actions, but also their spiritually. Worry is a sign a problem has not been fully surrendered to the Lord. It also reveals a need to develop a greater trust in God and Gods abilities. If Satan [Evil] can cause you to be fearful, filled with worry, anxiety, and self pity, then you will not be able to: 1] See God as God is, 2] Take your eyes off your circumstances, and 3] See your problem as a miracle opportunities. [Cerullo 1995, 58-62]

People often ask do all things really work together for my good? People often ask how can loss of a job, sickness, broken relationships, pending divorce, financial disaster be working for anyone's good. However, if you remember that the forces of EVIL - SATAN objective is to use circumstances to defeat you ... to steal, kill and destroy ... to bring sickness, financial problems and division ... and God will make you victorious in fighting EVIL-Satan and use these circumstances for your own good, then you will be able to face every circumstance without fear. You will develop a greater trust in God and God's miracle power. [Cerullo 1995, 63-64]

God does not immediately take you out of your circumstances, but uses your circumstance for your own good and transforms problems into miracles if you –

> *Refuse to accept your situation as it is. Lift your level of expectancy. Whatever your circumstance may be, you can face them without fear because you know that God wants to use your circumstances on your behalf.*
>
> *Begin each new day expecting a miracle. Believe God is working on your behalf. Praise God for it.*

Replace fear with courage ... worry with trust
... and doubt with a simply loyalty to God and God's
Word.
God will change your problems into
miracles. [Cerullo 1995, 69]

**REALIZE IN EVERY PROMISE OF GOD IS THE SEED OF
YOUR MIRACLE:** Miracles from their promise to their fulfillment, are
based upon God's promise to you, you must have a clear understanding
of Word of God. The Bible is God speaking to you. The Bible is God's
written word speaking to you and teaches you how to establish a personal
relationship with God, how to be happy and successful, raise a family, be
blessed financially, heal yourself and others. In the written Word, God
reveals God great love for you, and God's desire that all your needs are
met. Within God's written Word, God has given you many promises
which are called *miracle provisions.* [Cerullo 1995, 73 -75] Through these
miracle provisions, God provides for the healing of body, finances,
and family and provides comfort, peace and safety. For "all things,
whatsoever ye shall ask in prayer, ye shall receive" [The Bible, Matthew
21: 21 - 22].

God's promise is in God's Word which possesses the power for
its own fulfillment. God does not change and keeps God's Word. For
God declared :for I am the Lord, I change not ... [The Bible, Malchi 3:6].
God and God's word are one. In the beginning was God, and the Word
was God. All things were made by God and without God was not any
thing made that was made [The Bible, John 1:1-3]. God and his word are
inseparable. And since God does not change, God's word does not
change. [Cerullo 1995, 79]

God's promises are not dependent upon you. For God is a God
of purpose, plan, design and objectivity. God has a purpose for every
word, every promise. God does accomplish his purpose through God's
Word. The power for the fulfillment of God's promise, his miracle
provisions, is not in you. The seed or power for the fulfillment of God's
promise to you *is in the Word.* If God makes a promise to you, do not
give upon on God's promise for it will come to you no matter how long
you may have to wait. Before the Word of God can produce a miracle in
your life, you must first *receive it into your spirit.* Because the natural
mind is not capable of understanding miracles, God's Word, God's Promise
to you, must bypass your natural mind.

When people reach the place where it seems,
God's Promise, God's miracle provisions of healing,

deliverance, spiritual and financial prosperity are not being manifested in their lives, it is not because God's word is powerless; it is not necessarily because they do not have enough faith; it is because the Word has not penetrated into their spirit. The word of God [Living and Written] is a seed which must be planted deep within your spirit before it will grow and produce the miracle you need. [Cerullo 1995, 84]

God is a God of miracles and when God's sends the Word. God sends the faith and the power for the fulfillment. When that Word takes root within your spirit, the faith and power is released and the promise is fulfilled in your life.

Receive the spoken Word of God ... God's promises ... into your spirit and in total dependence upon God say, " Be it unto me as you have spoken."
[Cerullo 1995, 89]

PLANT A MIRACLE SEED - ACT ON GOD'S WORD: One you have received the promise within you spirit, *you must act upon it.* Although faith is a fact, it is also an act. The manifestation of a miracle is the direct results of the words of God spoken through you. In order for this to happen you must realign your thinking with God's word and speak forth God's word. That is you must plant the Word into your spirit and boldly speak it forth. [Cerullo 1995, 91-109] Because God has promised you:

They laid hands on the sick and they shall recover [The Bible 1995, 105]. I am the Lord that healeth thee [The Bible, Exodus 15:26]. With His strips I am healed [The Bible, Isaiah 53:5]. I will not worry about anything: in everything with prayer and thanksgiving I will make my requests known unto God. [The Bible, Philippians 4:6]

I will both lay me down in peace and sleep: for thou Lord, only makest me dwell in safety [Psalm 4:8]. The lord is my light and my salvation: whom shall I fear? The Lord is the strength of my life of whom shall I be afraid? [The Bible, Psalm 27:1] The Lord is on my side; I will not fear: What can man do unto me? [The Bible, Psalm 118:6] Behold, God is my salvation; I will trust, and not be afraid for the

> *Lord Jehovah is my strength and my song; he also*
> *becomes my salvation. [The Bible, Isaiah 12:2]*

Charismatic believe "a miracle is something that cannot happen by human means. It is supernatural invention of God in the affairs of your life." [Cerullo 1995, 166]   Miracles will happen for you if you follow the five steps: "1] See God as God is. 2] Take your eyes off your circumstances, 3] See your problems as miracle opportunities, 4] realize in every promise of God is the seed for your miracle, and 5] Plant a miracle seed ... act on God's Word." [Cerullo 1995, 166]

ENERGY HEALING

SPIRIT ENERGY - SOUND AND LIGHT: All sources of healing comes from energy. This energy is divine energy which descents to us during mediation. In the Christian tradition, it is called the Descent of the Holy Spirit; in Taoist Yoga, it is called the Descent of the Heaven Ki; in Kabalistic tradition - the Pillar of Light; in Indian Yoga - the spiritual bridge of light, or Antakharana. [Choa 1993, 24]   This is what is known as *spirit energy* which is both sound and light . All creatures and things in the cosmos are created in, form, and through waves of sound and light. Sound and light waves result in electromagnet currents. Electromagnetic current radiate to all directions of space and beyond.   Part of electromagnetic current is visible light, the light we can see with the physical organ of sight.

> *Electromagnetism is the product of an indefinable energy that underlines the physical forces of electricity, magnetism, light and heat. This energy is known as spiritual ether to the alchemists, "ain soph aur', or the "limitless light" to the Quabalists, "prana" or "prakitt" to the Hindus, and the "Great Spirit" or "Great Mystery" to the "Native American" or "spirit energy". [Elsbeth 1997, 52]*
>
> *Sound vibrations free up spirit energy with a sort of spiritual combustion not unlike physical combustion, which requires a spiritual sense, our breath is charged with spiritual energy; it carriers heat and light, and this is why we are able to produce sound and movement through out our body.   Our bodies are made up of electromagnetic currents and waves sound of light.[Elsbeth 1997, 52]*
>
> *Whether the behavior of light is viewed from an esoteric or exoteric standpoint, we find the following holds true: 1] Light disperses throughout the cosmos and pervades all of space. 2] Everything is made up or reciprocal with the electromagnetic frequencies of which light is a part. 3] Every substance in the universe is connect to light in its essential composition. [Elsbeth 1997, 53]]*

All forms originate out of sound and color is the visual translation of sound. As a result of their frequencies carried by sound the forms and movement of light waves may vary resulting in light waves producing color. "Color is the vibratory motion of refracted sound waves reflecting myriad forms of spirit energy in our field of perception" [Elsbeth 1997, 54].

There is a precise harmony between specific notes or tones corresponding to the musical scale and the sum total of vibrations per second which transfer the feeling of a specific color to the sight center in the eyes. Also, the ears actually emit as well as receive sound, while the brain has a holographic way of processing sound. [Talbot 1991, 292-293] This is the reason visually impaired individuals can feel color, even though they cannot see it. Also, the reason people who are deaf in one ear can locate the source of sound without moving theirs heads. [Elsbeth 1997, 54]

There is evidence that the human body radiates varying waves of light which correspond to the color spectrum from infrared to ultraviolet waves. The essential wavelength of every cell and every organ within the body its own particular color and tone. The human body acts as a prism. When light passes in and through it the body-prism, some people see a rainbow of color called an *aura*. [Smith 1997, 2-7] An aura is an etheric matrix consisting of several distinct waves of light that surround the physical body. The aura can have the appearance of a luminous mist or cloud. Through looking at a persons aura is possible to judge the conditions of the body, mind and emotions because aura radiates heat and light [electromagnetism] from the inter core of the body which displays our life essence. The aura gives us a picture of the level of electromagnetic energy generated from within the body. [Elsbeth 1997, 56]

Spiritual traditions have at their core a metaphor for brining the aura life essence back into balance. These traditions brining the body-earth back to nature by raising the serpent power. This power is known as the Kundalini or light force which is found like a coiled serpent that can be activity to move through the body centers known as Spirit Energy centers or charkas. [Elsbeth 1997, 58].

NEGATIVE SPACE/TIME ENERGY - FASTER THAN THE SPEED OF LIGHT: This Spirit Energy is light and all matter is made up of frozen light. Frozen light can be viewed as miniature energy interference patterns or microcosmic energy fields occupying an infinitesimal space. When one delves into the subatomic world of particle physics the illusion of solidity melts away and in fact the atom is mostly made up of empty space. The minute particles that fill this void are frozen packets of light. Matter is composed of highly complex, infinitely orchestrated energy fields. Matter is made up of fields within fields. If we apply this to living systems, the cellular matrix of the physical body can be seen as a complex energetic interference pattern interpenetrated by organizing bio-energetic field of the etheric body. Matter is specialized energy fields and also is type of energy interference pattern. [Gerber 1998, 59]

At the quantum level of sub-atomic particles, all matter is literally frozen, particular energy fields [i.e. frozen light]. Complex aggregates of ·matter [i.e. molecules] are really specialized energy fields. Both light and matter have frequency characteristic. The high frequency of matter, the less dense and more subtle the matter. The etheric body is composed of matter of higher frequency than physical matter and is referred as subtle matter. The universe itself [God] may be a tremendous energy interference pattern with the characteristic of a hologram. By decoding a small piece of the Universal Hologram, one may unfold information about the whole universe stored within the matrix. The selective focus of consciousness via psychic attunement may hold the potential for decoding the Universal Hologram [God]. If one were to view God as all there is, then, through the holographic inter-connective of space, God could simultaneously be in contact with all creations. For example some psychics who have the ability to do remote viewing have the ability to tap in and decode their own piece of the Cosmic Hologram. It is believed that mediation and other mental disciplines may condition or program the physical and subtle energetic hardware of our sophisticated nervous systems to gain access to high levels of information. Achieving such specialized states of consciousness allow an individual to gain access to hierarchical levels of information enfolded within the structure of matter/energy field and space itself. Expanded human awareness may be the most important tool for exploring the holographic universe and the multidimensional human being. [Gerber 1988 57-69]

As we learn more about energy, we realize that consciousness is a form of energy. The higher states of consciousness can be used to bring energy to a specific location. This localized energy can be used for healing. This is calling upon the God consciousness as form of energy to channel through us and to use this energy for healing. Our illness may be a symbolic reflection of our own internal states of emotional unrest, spiritual blockage, and dis-ease. Our subtle energetic components that is chakras and meridian systems, translate our emotional and spiritual difficulties into physiological weaknesses which may eventual result in localized systems breakdown in the physical body that is disease. When disease occurs, it is a sign that we are constricting the natural flow of creative consciousness and subtle life energies through our multi-dimensional body/mind/spirit complex. It is an indicator that something has going wrong with the system and the system must be re-balanced if lasting health is to be obtained. Many of the basic emotions/spiritual issues which we are trying to work through are reflected in key lesions of the chakras. These chakras issues relate to grounding, sexuality, personal power, love, will creative expression, inner vision, and spiritual seeking. When there is a blockage in working through one of these key life issues, it can result in the blockage of the flow of energy in the corresponding chakra to the aforesaid issues. This can constrict the flow of life energy to the associated body organ system[s]. The blockage can express itself in illness both mental and physical. [Gerber 1998, 464, 500 & 501].

Many wonder what is the energy which comes from God, from the Cosmos, it is a divine energy which travels faster than the speed of light. It is best described by the TELL - EINSTEIN MODEL which is a scientific model of positive and negative space/time domains which are predicted by the relativistic version of Einstein's mass/energy equation. According to Dr. William Tiller, the leading proponent of the model, positive space/ time energy and substance vibrate at speeds less than or near the speed of light, and have electrical or electromagnetic qualities. Negative space/time energy and substance vibrate or move at speed faster than light, are magnetic in quality, and are of an energetic mature refereed to as magneto-electric. [Gerber 1988, 542] The properties of particles traveling at supraluminial [faster-than-light] velocities are very interesting. That is positive space/time matter is associated with the forces of electricity and electromagnetic [EM] radiation, negative space/time matter is associated primarily with magnetism and the force which Teller describes as magneto-electric [ME] radiation. In addition, negative space/time particles have negative mass and demonstrate the property of negative entropy. Entropy is a term which the tendency towards the disorder of a system. The greater the entropy, the greater the disorder. In general most systems within the physical universe ten towards increasing positive entropy and more disorder over time., that is things tend to fall apart. The behavior of living systems is the exception to the aforesaid rule. Biological systems take in raw materials [food] and organize these simple components into complex macro-molecular structures [such as protein, DNA, collagen, etc.]. Living systems display the property of negative entropy, or a tenancy towards decreasing the disorder of the systems. They take in substances which are broken down to elements which are less organized, and then build them up into systems which are more organized. Living organisms take in raw materials and *ENERGY* and self- organize them into complex structural and physiologic sub-components. One might say than that *life-force* seems to be associated with the negative entropy characteristic. When the body dies the *life-*

force vacates the physical forms, the reaming unoccupied shell returns, via earthly microorganisms, to its raw constituents, in characteristic positive entropy fashion. The etheric body, a self-organizing holographic energy template, also demonstrates negative entropic properties. The etheric body supplies the spatial ordering properties to the cellular systems of the physical body. This is the negatively entropic characteristic of the subtle life energies, that is the etheric, astral, mental and causal bodies. In addition, the negative space/time matter is primary magnetic in nature. The energetic fields of healers fit Dr. Tillers criteria for negative/ space substance, or magneto-electric energy. In that they demonstrate certain qualitative similarities to magnetic fields. Also, they have negative entropic properties, that is the ability to reassemble disordered molecules such as enzymes. [Gerber 1988, 145-149]

MAGNETIC LIFE FORCE ENERGY: The laying-on-of-hands healing has been practiced throughout the world for thousands of years. Franz Mesmer in the late 1700s theorized that a subtle life-energy of magnetic nature was exchanged between healers and patient during land-on-hands. Also, he discovered water could store this subtle force for transfer to sick patients in need of healing. Dr. Bernard Grad in the 1960s replicated Mesmer's findings. Dr. Justa Smith healers could also repair damaged enzymes which demonstrated the principal that healing energy was negatively entropic in nature, that is it caused systems to become more ordered. Also, he found healers could produce the effect on non-living chemical systems. Dr. Dolores Krieger's research demonstrated that healer's energies could increase hemoglobin levels in patients similar to the way that they increase chlorophyll content in healer-treated plants. Also, Dr. Krieger demonstrated that people could be trained to do healing, that is healing is an innate human potential and it can be a learned skill. [Gerber 1998, 385-318 & 323-324]

The laying-on-hands healing is more accurately described as magnetic healing. It is works at the physical-etheric levels of re-balancing, and it is performed with the healers hands in close proximity to the patient. Spiritual healers usually work with many levels of mind and spirit as well at the level of the body. The nature of the higher dimensional energy is that it transcends all limitations of time and space by virtue of the fact that levels from etheric and higher energies are in the domain of negative space/time. As such the energies working at these levels move in dimension which is outside the usual reference of ordinary [or positive] space/time to which the conscious mind is limited in its perception. Additionally, the frequency at which spiritual healing takes place often extend to the same level at which the Higher-Self exist and operates. [Gerber 1998, 319 & 323-324]

PRANIC HEALING

Pranic healer believe that the body is made of two parts: the visible physical body and the unseen invisible energy body called the bioplasmic body. The physical body is that part of the human body which we see, touch and are the most acquainted. The bioplasmic body is invisible luminous energy which interpenetrates the visible physical body and extends four to five inches. This energy is called the etheric body or etheric double by clairvoyants. Panic healing is defined as the ancient science and art of healing which utilizes prana, ki or vital energy to heal the whole physical body, mind, soul and spirit. Panic healing involves the manipulation of ki and bioplasmic matter of the patient's body. It has also been called psychic healing, magnetic healing, faith healing, ki healing, vitalic healing and the laying on of hands. [Choa 1990, 1]

PRANA OR KI - THE VITAL ENERGY OF LIFE FORCE:
Prana or ki is the vital energy of life force that keeps the body health and alive. It is also know as the breath of life. *Miraculous healings* occur when the healer projects Prana, vital energy, or the breath of life to the patient thereby healing the patient. there are three major sources of Prana. Solar Prana is Prana from sunlight. It invigorates the whole body and promotes good health. Solar Prana can be obtain by exposure to sunlight or sunbathing and by drinking water that has been exposed to sunlight. Prolonged exposure or to much solar Prana will harm the whole body because it is very potent. Prana contained in the air is called air Prana or air vitality globule. Air Prana is absorbed by the lungs through breathing and directly by the energy centers in the bioplasmic body. These energy centers are called chakras. More air can be absorbed by deep slow rhythmic breathing than be short breathing. It can be also absorbed the pores of the skin by people who have undergone certain training. Prana contained in the ground is ground Prana or ground vitality globule. This is absorb through the soles of the feet. It is done automatically and unconsciously. Walking barefoot increase the amount of ground Prana absorbed by the body. One can learn to consciously draw in more Prana to increase vitality, capacity to do more work, and ability to think more clearly. Water absorbs Prana from sunlight, air, and the ground. Plants and trees absorb Prana from sunlight, air, water, and the ground. People and animals absorb Prana from sunlight, air, ground, water, and food [fresh food contains more Prana than preserved food]. [Choa 1990 1-3]

CREATION OF MIRACLES THROUGH PRANA HEALING - THE ROLE OF JESUS THE SHAMAN: In *The Essene of the Gospel of Peace,* we learn that Jesus the Christ was very knowledgeable of *Prana*

Healing and used it to create *miracles*. We also realize that Jesus was a Shaman. A Shaman deals with the elements of forces of Air, Fire, Water, and Earth. All the energies of all the worlds spin like wheels on the Shaman's path. The upper world of the sky journeys, the lower worlds of the earth journeys and the middle world of humankind all connect on the path of the Shaman. All worlds spin and vibrate for the Shaman. The Shaman rides the wheel of each world to feel its vibration and direct power. This is the wisdom of the Shaman. The Shaman must experience the worlds of the riding wheels of vibrations. This will bring the attunements with the deep shamanic energies of nature. The Shaman remains rooted in personal connection to the earth by staying centered· and balance in the midst of the chaos of spinning wheels of energy and vibration. A Shaman is able to reach into the spirit from the connection with the Earth. "In this way, the Shaman becomes channel between the energies of the earth and Nature and the energies of Spirit. Like a living tree, the Shaman is rooted deep in the earth, reaching and growing into Spirit. The Shaman is an Earth connection; the Shaman is connect to Spirit." - God. [Wolfe 1997, xiii]

The cry of over 2,000 years ago was Master heal us! This was the cry of the masses to Jesus, for they knew that Jesus had the power to heal all manner of *dis-ease.* Jesus replied, "I will lead you into the kingdom of our mother's angels, where the power of Satan [disease] cannot enter". They asked, "who is our Mother and who are her angles and where is her kingdom?" Jesus replied,

> *Your Mother is in you and you in her. If you receives your Mother's angels and you obey her laws, you shall have no disease, for the power of the Earthy Mother is above all. The power will destroy Satan and his Kingdom, and has rule over all your bodies and all living things. ... The blood which runs in us is born of our Earthy Mother. The air which we breathe is born of the breath of the earthly Mother .... Man is the son of the Earth Mother and from her did man receive the whole body. ... For your breath is her breath; your blood is her blood; your bones are her bones; your flesh is her flesh; your bowels her bowels; your eyes are your ears are her eyes and ears. ... The Earth Mother protects the Son of Man from all dangers and from all evils." [Szekely 1978, 9-11]*

Jesus said, " Seek the fresh air of the forest and of the fields, and there in the midst of them shall you find the angel of air. Put off your shoes and your clothing and suffer the angle of air to embrace all of your body. Then breath long and deep, that the angel of air may be brought within you. I tell you truly, the angel of air shall cast out your body all unclearness which defiled it *without and within*. Truly *all must be born again* by air and by truth, for your body breathes the air of the Earthly Mother, and your spirit breathes the truth of the Heavenly Father." [Szekely 1978, 14-15]

Also, Jesus said, "Seek the angel of sunlight and water in the same manner as the angel of air". Then, Jesus "pointed with his hand to where the running of the water and the sun's heat had soften the clayed mud earth by the edge of the water. Sink your feet in the mire, that embrace the angel of earth may draw out of you bones all uncleanness and all disease. And you will see Satan and your pains fly from the embrace of the angel of earth. And the knots of your bones will vanish away, and they will be straightened, and all your pains will disappear." [Szekely 1978, 16-30] " Come and breath in by your mouth the strength of the angels of water, sunshine, and air, that it may come into your body and cast out Satan from you". [Szekley 1978, 32] Jesus said, "Upon casting out Satan fill you body with the Angel of God and rededicate them as temples of God". [Szekley 1978, 31]. Jesus state, " Give thanks not to me but to your Earthy Mother, who sent you her healing angels. Go, and sin no more, that you may never again see disease. And let the healing Angeles become your guardians. [Szekely 1978, 36]

Jesus stated that in order to be without disease, "Honor they Heavenly Father and they earthly Mother, and do their commandments, that thy days may be long on earth" And then he gave his the greatest commandment: "Love the Lord they God with all they heart, and with all they soul, and with all they strength: this is the first and greatest commandment. And the second is like unto it: Love they neighbor as thyself. There is none other commandment greater than these." [Szekely 1978, 36-37]

> *Jesus said " be true sons of God, that you also may partake in his power and in knowledge of all secrets. for wisdom can only come from love of God, Love, therefore, your Heavenly Father and your Earthly Mother with all your heart, and with all your spirit. And serve them, that their angels may serve you also. Let all your deeds be scarified to God. And feed not Satan, for the wages of sin is death. But with God lies*

the reward of the good, his love, which is knowledge
and power of eternal life. [Szekely 1978, 35]

Jesus was one of the greatest healers of all times. The energies which flowed from him cured the body, mind, soul, and spirit. Jesus stated that there was no mystery to being a healer like him. Everyone can heal if the have faith and believe in God that God can create miracles. We get most of our vital energy from the air we breath. For "Then the Lord God formed man out of the dust of the ground and breathed into his nostrils the breath of life, and man became a living being. [The Bible, Genesis 2:7]

SEVEN STEPS TO THE MIRACLE OF PRANA HEALING [BREATH OF LIFE]: The miracle of pranic healing is created through the use breath of life of the ki or vital energy. The seven basic steps in pranic healing our: 1] Sensitizing the hands, 2] Scanning the inner aura, 3] Sweeping [cleansing]: general and localized, 4] Increasing the receptivity. of the patient, 5] Energizing with prana, 6] Stabilizing the projected pranic energy, 7] Releasing the projected pranic energy or detaching. [Choa 1993, 10]

In pranic psychotherapy, there are four additional healing techniques: 1] Removing and is integrating traumatic psychic energy, negative though entities, negative psychic entities, and negative elements [an advance cleansing technique]. 2] Disintegrating negative elements and sealing the creaks or holes in the etheric or protective webs [An advanced form of energizing]. 3] Activating and inhibiting the chakras [Also, an advance form of energizing]. 4] Creating a positive image of the patient or a positive thought entity for the patient. [Choa 1993, 11]

Prance healing is energy healing. Energy is brought into the healers body, mind. soul, and spirit through mediation and breathing exercisers. The energy is drawn from the air, water, earth and living things such as trees. This energy is concentrated in the healer and released through the chakras in the healer's hand. The energy is used to balance the patient's chokers and remove negative energies from the patient's body, mind, soul and spirit. These negative energies are found in the chakras found in the patient's physical body, etheric, mind and causal bodies [that is the patients' aura]. The negative energies are removed from the patient by the healer and then the healer fills the patient's chakras with healing energy such as a golden white light energy. [Choa 1990, 39 -49]

THE CHAKRAS AND THEIR RELATIONSHIP TO HEALING ENERGIES: To understand the role of the healer it is necessary to understand the functions of the chakras in their relationship to healing energies. Our first understanding will be in terms of the relationship of the chakras to our psychological functions.

The major chakras (or energy centers) control and energize the internal organs and also control and affect one's psychological conditions. In other words, they' are centers for certain psychological functions. The chakras control our emotions as illustrated by the following:

1) Basic chakra. This energy center is located at the base of the spine. The basic chakra is the center of self-prevention or instinct of survival. People who are depressed or suicidal have depleted and under-activated basic chakras. People who have lost touch with physical reality, or who have become quiet unrealistic, also have depleted basic chakras. People who, in spite of their qualifications and relatively good health, have difficulty getting jobs have partly depleted or under-activated basic chakras.

2) Sex chakra. This energy center is located in the pubic area. It is the center of the sexual instinct. People with strong sex chakras usually have strong sex drives.

3) Naval chakra. This energy center is located on the navel. It is the center of the "instinct of knowing"."

4) Meng Mein chakra. This energy center is located at the back of the navel. It has something to do with the upward flow of pranic energy from the basic chakra. Patients who are violent have over-activated meng mein chakras. This energy center should only be handled by experienced or advanced pranic healers. In infants, this chakra should not be energized because of possible harmful effects. With children, older patients, and pregnant women, it is also not advisable to energize this chakra because of possible negative reactions. It is better to avoid unnecessary risks.

5) Spleen Chakra. The front spleen chakra is located on the center of the left lowermost front rib. In other words, it is located just below the left breast. The back spleen chakra is located at the back of the front spleen chakra. People who are depressed have depleted spleen chakras.

6) Solar plexus chakra. The front solar plexus is located at the hollow area between the front ribs. The back solar plexus is located at the back of the front solar plexus chakra. The solar plexus chakra is the center of lower emotions, such as anger, hate, irritation, resentment, worry, anxiety, tension, fear selfishness, aggressiveness, abrasives, addiction, and the like. "when people are physically violent, the ajna, solar plexus, basic, and meng mein chakras become over-activated. But the main chakra that influences the other chakras is the solar plexus chakra. By normalizing (through cleansing and energizing) this chakra, violent people can be calmed down in a short period. In healing psychological ailments, this chakra is almost always treated. It is also the center of courage, daring, perseverance, and the desire to win.

7) Heart chakra. The front heart chakra is located in front of the heart or at the center of the chest. The back heart chakra is located at the back of the heart. The heart chakra is the center of higher emotions such as peace, serenity, joy, compassion, loudness, gentleness, tenderness, caring, consideration, patience, and sensitivity By activating the heart chakra, the lower emotional energies can be transmuted into higher forms of emotional energies. This is why psychologically ill patients must do the Meditation on Twin Hearts twice a day for several months. It will be better if they can do it daily for the rest of their lives. In acupuncture, hysterical people can be calmed down by stimulating certain acupuncture points which also activate the heart chakra.

8) Throat chakra. This is located at the center of the throat. It is the center of the lower mental faculty, the concrete mind. It is used when meticulous details are involved, like studying, planning, painting, and the like. It is also the center of higher creativity while the sex chakra is the center of "physical creativity" or procreation. When the throat chakra is quite strong and active, the sex chakra is also quite active. This is why creative artists have strong sexual drives.

9) Ajna chakra. This is located between the eyebrows. It is the center of higher mental faculty -abstract mind- and is also the "directing center" or the "will center".

10) Forehead chakra. This chakra controls the nervous system and is the center of lower buddhic or cosmic consciousness.

11) Crown chakra. This chakra is located at the crown (or top) of the head. It controls the brain and is the center of higher buddhic faculty or higher cosmic consciousness. The buddhic faculty (when fully developed) manifests as "direct knowing or perception." It is knowing without need to study". What is learned through the buddhic faculty in a few minutes will require weeks, if not months, to put into words. One with only a developmental faculty will have to plow or muddle through a problem, whereas another with even only a partly developed buddhic faculty has a quick overall grasp of the problem and the possible solutions. The mental faculty is then used to check on the validity of the solution and to "materialize" that solution. Unfortunately, our present educational system does not encourage the development of the buddhic faculty on the grounds that it provides an answers that are not materialistic in nature.

Mental faculty can be compared to a blind man, while the buddhic faculty can be compared to a person who can see. In order for a blind man to have an idea of the shape of an elephant, he has to spend considerable time touching the elephant and trying to deduce and synthesize the data gathered, while one who can see will immediately know that shape. Buddhic consciousness is understanding the subject matter not after a long period of study nor through inductive or deductive reasoning, but through immediate and direct comprehension or perception. [Choa 1993, 2-6]

Another detailed understanding of the chakras and esoteric healing is presented by Zachary F. Lansdowne, Ph.D. who stated the following:

The emotional and mental bodies also have force centers that are counterparts of the centers in the etheric body. That is chakras which are etheric force center.

Each of the seven major chakras vitalizes its nearby area of the physical body, both etheric and dense portions, including minor chakras and dense organs.. The health of an organ is viewed as dependent on the condition of its associated chakra, for example, whether the chakra is balanced, over-stimulated, or under-stimulated.

A major chakra evolves over time and moves from a sluggish semi-dormant state to an active fully developed state. When a chakra develops, it gains the ability to work, with additional forces and to perform additional functions. Following are summaries of some of the functions of each of the seven major chakras, plus the splenic chakra, in both undeveloped and developed states:

THE CROWN CHAKRA vitalizes the cerebrum (or upper brain) and anchors the consciousness stream from the causal body- When developed, it registers wisdom from the causal body, insights from the spiritual mind, and dedication for selfless service from the spiritual will.

THE BROW CHAKRA vitalizes the cerebellum (or lower brain) and central nervous system (which consists of nerve fibers within the brain stem and spinal cord). When developed, this chakra focuses wisdom, insights, and dedication for selfless service (all received via the crown chakra),. which then can be used to control and dominate the personality. The brow is not the organ of creation in the same sense that the throat center is, but instead it expresses the intention to create that lies behind active creativity.

THE THROAT CHAKRA vitalizes the lungs and vocal apparatus, and it also registers concrete thoughts from the mental body (received via the solar plexus chakra). When developed, the throat chakra responds to strength and clarity from the causal body (received via the brow chakra), enabling creativity to be expressed in thought, speech, and writing.

THE HEART CHAKRA anchors the life stream (sutratma) from the monad, and this stream controls the circulation of blood, which in turn feeds the individual cells of the body. This chakra both vitalizes and controls the vagus nerve, the largest nerve in the parasympathetic nervous system (which activates involuntary muscles that restore the body's energy). When developed, it registers compassion from the spiritual love, which is experienced as a sense of oneness with others.

THE SOLAR PLEXUS CHAKRA vitalizes the sympathetic nervous system (which activates involuntary muscles that mobilize the body for action). This chakra is considered to be developed in an average or ordinary human being, in which case it registers emotions that can incorporate both feelings from the emotional body and concrete thoughts from the mental body.

THE SPLENIC CHAKRA assimilates prana from the atmosphere, which then vitalizes the entire system of major and minor chakras. It is considered to be in a developed state for all human beings.

THE SACRAL CHAKRA vitalizes the sexual life and organs of reproduction. It also is considered to be developed.

THE BASIC CHAKRA vitalizes the kidneys. This chakra also feeds the life-giving principle, the will to live, to all parts of the physical body, resulting in the fundamental instinct of self-preservation. When developed, it allows the dedication for selfless service from the spiritual will to be registered continually by the crown chakra.   As indicated by the foregoing list, only the crown, heart, and solar plexus chakras can directly receive energies from higher planes. Any other chakra can receive a higher plane energy only after the energy has initially been registered by one of these three chakras.   Because each major chakra can vitalize or control a 'portion of the dense body, it might be expected that a person who has developed a particular chakra would display some abnormality in the activity of his associated organs, in the sense this activity would somehow be different from that of a person with an undeveloped chakra. Although contemporary science is unable to detect the presence of a chakra directly, it may be possible with contemporary instruments to detect differences in the activity of organs associated with a chakra In this way it may be possible to draw inferences as to the physiological effects of chakra development and whether a particular chakra is or is not developed. [Lansdowne 1986, 15-17]

Also, Motoyama has reported experimental research which supports the aforesaid hypothesis of Lansdowne. He showed that there were several physiological differences among a group of individuals said to have developed their heart chakra when compared to another group not having this development. [Motoyama 1978, 90-93, 143-144]

THE RELATIONSHIP OF CHAKRAS TO ORGANS, ENDOCRINE GLANDS AND DISEASES: To have a clear understanding as to the way healing function, it is necessary to have an understanding of the chakra system and how each chakra affect a different part of the physical body. Such an understanding can be obtained through a review of the following chart [Choa 1990, 96-97]:

SEE ILLUSTRATION PAGE 64

There, also, is a relationship between the chakras and the endocrine glands. "A gland is defined as endocrine if it forms a specific substance and secretes this substance into the blood and if this substance exerts a specific effect on some organ or process are a distance from the gland. The specific substance is called a hormone, and it can be viewed as being a chemical messenger from the gland to the target organ or process." [Lansdowne 1986, 20]. These glands are consider to be the dense physical counterparts of the charkas. That is the physical form are the crystallized counterparts and instruments for the chakras. [Chaney 1966, 11] A healer can cause a change in the endocrine gland system by stimulating the chakras with healing energies which will cause a healing throughout the body and/or a specific area of the body. The following charts show the relationships between the chakras and the endocrine glands [Lansdowne 1986, 21-23]:

ASSOCIATION BETWEEN ETHERIC CHAKRAS AND ENDOCRINE GLANDS, ACCORDING TO VARIOUS SOURCES

ASSOCIATED ENDOCRINE GLANDS

Chakra *Gardner*	*Bailey* *Schwarz*	*Beasley*	*Chaney*
Crown	Pineal	Pineal	Pineal
Brow	Pituitary	Pituitary	Pituitary
Throat	Thyroid	Thyroid	Thyroid
Heart	Thymus	Thymus	Thymus
Solar plexus	Pancreas	Adrenals	Liver
Splenic	Spleen	Spleen	Spleen
Sacral	Gonads	Gonads	Gonads
Basic	Adrenals	Adrenals	Gonads, pituitary gonads

THE CHAKRAS, THE CORRESPONDING ORGANS AND POSSIBLE DISEASES

CHAKRA	LOCATION	FUNCTIONS AND CORRESPONDING ORGANS	DISEASES
1. Crown chakra	Crown of head	Brain and pineal gland.	Diseases related to the pineal gland and the brain (physical or psychological illnesses).
2. Forehead chakra	Center of the forehead	Nervous system and pineal gland.	Loss of memory, paralysis and epilepsy.
3. Ajna chakra	Between the eyebrows	Pituitary gland and endocrine glands;	Controls the other major chakras. Cancer, allergy, asthma, and diseases related to the endocrine glands.
4. Throat chakra	Center of the throat	Throat, thyroid and parathyroid glands.	Throat-related illnesses likegoiter, sore throat, loss of voice, asthma, etc.
5. Heart chakra:			
a) Front heart	Center of the chest	Meant, thymus gland, and the circulatory system.	Heart and circulatory ailments.
b) Back heart	Back of the heart	Lungs, and to a certain degree, the heart.	Lung ailments.
6. Solar plexus chakra:			
a) Front solar:	Solar plexus area	Acts as an energy clearing house center. It also controls the heating and cooling system of thebody. Pancreas, liver, diaphragm,large intestine, appendix, stomach, Small intestine and to a certain degree other internal organs and other parts of the body.	High cholesterol, diabetes, ulcer, hepatitis, rheumatoid arthritis, heart ailments and other illnesses.
b) Back solar:	Opposite the front solar	It has the same function as the plexus chakra.	
7. Spleen chakra:			
a) Front spleen	Spleen	Major entry point for air prana between the front solar plexus or air vitality globule, energizes chakra and the navel chakra. The other major chakra and the It is located at the middle part of the left bottom rib.	Low vitality, weak body, and blood ailments.
b) Back spleen	Back part of the abdomen		
	Back of the front spleen	It has similar functions with the front spleen chakra.	

72

THE CHAKRAS, THE CORRESPONDING ORGANS AND POSSIBLE DISEASES

CHAKRA	LOCATION	FUNCTIONS AND CORRESPONDING ORGANS	DISEASES
8. Navel chakra	Navel	Small and large intestine.	Constipation, difficulty in giving birth, appendicitis, low vitality and other diseases related to the intestines.
9. Meng mein	Back of the navel	Kidneys, adrenal glands; energizes to a certain degree other internal organs; controls blood pressure.	Kidney problems, low vitality, high blood pressure and back problems.
10. Sex chakra	Pubic area	Sexual organs, bladder and legs: it is the lower or physical creative center.	Sex-related problems and bladder ailments.
11. Basic chakra	Base of the spine	Adrenal glands and sex organs; it energizes the physical body-bones, muscles, blood, and internal organs; affects general vitality, body heat, and the growth of infants and children; center of self-survival or self-preservation.	Cancer, leukemia, low vitality, allergy, asthma, sexual ailments, back problems, blood ailments, growth problems and psychological disorders.

FUNCTIONS OF THE ENDOCRINE GLANDS

GLAND HORMONE	FUNCTION OR EFFECT
Anterior Pituitary Thyrotropic (TSH)	Stimulates the thyroid gland to secrete its hormones.
Adrenocorticotropic (ACTH)	Stimulates the adrenal center to produce its hormones.
Melanoocyte-stimulating hormone (MSH)	Function in man is uncertain.
Follicle-stimulating hormone	Stimulates the maturation of the ovum and production of estrogen in the female. Stimulates sperm development in the male.
Luteinizing hormone (LH)	Triggers release of the mature ovum and production of rogesterone and estrogen in the female. Stimulates testosterone secretion in the male.
Lactogenic hormone (LTH)	Stimulates milk production in the female. Also acts like growth hormone.
Growth hormone	Controls general body growth and affects fat, protein, and carbohydrate metabolism.
Posterior Pituitary	Oxytocin, Stimulates the contraction of uterine muscles during birth and causes ejection of milk.
Vasopressin	Primary control of water reabsorption from the kidney tubule and causes contraction of smooth muscles.
Hypothalamus	Neurohormones, Triggers the release of pituitary tropic hormones.
Adrenal cortex	Cortisone and cortisol. Help control glucose-glycogen balances, water balance, protein utilization, and general metabolism.

Aldosterone	Controls mineral balance, mainly sodium and potassium.
Adrenal medulla	Epinephrine. Excites the nervous system, circulatory system, and increases release of glucose from the liver.
Norepinephrine	Increases metabolic rate, constricts blood vessels.
Thyroid Thyroxine	Controls carbohydrate metabolism.
Parathyroid	Parathormone. Regulates calcium and potassium metabolism.
Pancreas	Insulin. Increases glycogen storage in the liver, decreases blood sugar, affects water balance, primary factor in regulating glucose passages into cells.
Glucagon	Stimulates release of glucose from the liver.
Ovary	Estrogen. Initiate preparation of the uterus for fertilized egg, stimulate and maintain female secondary sex characteristics.
Progesterone	Necessary to prevent abortion of the embryo and stimulate final preparation of the uterus for the fertilized egg.
Placenta	Chorionic gonadotropin. Acts with other female sex hormones to maintain pregnancy.
Ovary & Placenta	Relaxin. Relaxes the ligaments of the pelvis to enlarge the birth canal passage.
Testes	Androgen. Stimulates and maintains male secondary sex characteristics
Digestive tract	Secretin. Stimulates the release of pancreatic juice.

We can understanding by reading and processing the information in the foregoing pages and charts is that the esoteric healer can act as a catalyst to healing by moving energy in, out and through the chakras which affects the secretion of hormones that directly affect the healing process in the human body. In chemistry a catalyst is defined as a substance that remains unchanged while increasing the rate of reaction between other substances. For instances, enzymes act as catalysts in the digestion of food, enabling chemical changes to take place in their presence. Although we must heal ourselves, the healing process can be facilitated by the catalytic presence of an esoteric healer. [Lansdowne 1986, 12]

MEDITATIONS WHICH BRING HEALING ENERGIES TO THE HEALER:

Throughout the centuries healers have used various techniques to bring energy to themselves which they used to heal others and the world. One of the best meditation techniques for bring this energy to you, the healer, is described by Choa Kok Sui in his Meditation on the Twin Hearts. This is a wonderful technique for bring energy into the body and is described as follows:

MEDITATIONS OF THE TWIN HEARTS

THE ILLUMINATION TECHNIQUE, or Meditation on the Twin Heart, is a technique to achieve Buddhic Consciousness or cosmic conscious or illumination. It is also a form of service to the world because the world is harmonized to a certain degree by blessing the entire earth with loving kindness.

Meditation on the Twin Hearts is based on the principle that some of the major chakras are entry points or gateways to certain levels or horizons of consciousness. To achieve illumination or Buddhic conscious, it is necessary to fully activate the crown chakra. The crown chakra, when frilly activated, becomes like a cup. To be ore exact, the twelve inner petals open and turn upward like a cup to receive spiritual energies which are distributed to other parts of the body. The crowns worn by kings and queens are but poor physical replicas or symbols of the indescribably resplendent crown chakra of a fully-developed person. The fully activated crown chakra is symbolized as the Holy Grail.

The crown chakra can only be fully activated when the heart chakra is first fully activated. The heart chakra is a replica of the crown chakra. When you look at the heart chakra, it looks like the inner chakra of the crown chakra, which has twelve golden petals. The heart chakra is the lower correspondence of the crown chakra. The crown chakra is the center of illumination and divine love or oneness with all. To explain what is divine love and illumination to an ordinary person is just like trying to explain what color is to a blind man. The heart chakra is the center of higher emotions. It is the center for compassion, joy, affection, consideration, mercy and other refined emotions. Without developing higher refined emotions, how can one possibly experience divine love?

There are many ways of activating the heart and crown chakras. One can use physical movements, hatha yoga, yoga breathing techniques, mantras or words of power and visualization techniques All. of these techniques are effective but are not fast enough. One of the most effective and fastest ways to activate these chakras is to do meditation on loving-kindness or to bless the whole earth with loving-kindness. By using the heart chakra and the crown chakra in blessing the earth with loving-kindness, they become channels for spiritual energies; thereby becoming activated in the process. By blessing the earth with loving-kindness, you at doing a form of world service, and by blessing the earth with loving-kindness, you are in turn blessed many times. It is in blessing that you are blessed. It is in giving that you receive. That is the law!

A person with a fully activated crown chakra does not necessarily a have illumination for he or she has yet to learn how to make use of the crown chakra to achieve illumination. It is just like having a sophisticated computer but not knowing how to operate it. Once the crown chakra has been fully activated, then you have to do meditation on the light, on the mantra Aum [Sanskrit for the Supreme Being] and on the gap between the two Aums. Intense concentration should be focused not only on the mantra Aum but especially on the gap between the two Aums. It is by fully and intensely concentrating rating on the light and the gap between the two Aums that illumination, or samadhi, is achieved !

With most people, their other chakras are quite activated. The basic chakra, sex chakra and solar plexus chakra are activated in practically all people. With these people, their instincts for self-survival, their sex drive and their tendency to react with their lower emotions are very active. With the pervasiveness of modern education and work that requires the use of the mental faculty, the ajna chakra and the throat chakra are developed in a lot of people What is not developed in most people are the heart and crown chakras. Modern education, unfortunately, tends to over-emphasize the development of the throat chakra and the ajna chakra or the development of the concrete mind and the abstract mind. The development of the heart has been neglected. Because of this, you may encounter people who are quite intelligent but very abrasive. This type of person has not yet matured emotionally or the heart chakra is quite underdeveloped. Though he or she is intelligent and may be successful, human relationships are poor; with hardly any friends and no family or a broken family. By using the meditation on the two hearts, a person becomes harmoniously balanced.

Whether the abstract and concrete mind will be used constructively or destructively depends upon the development of the heart. When the solar plexus chakra is overdeveloped and the heart chakra is underdeveloped, or when the lower emotions are active and the higher emotions ate underdeveloped, then the mind would probably be used destructively. Without the development of the heart in most people, world peace will be an unattainable dream. This is why the development of the heart should be emphasized in the educational system.

People less than 18 years old should not practice the illumination technique since the body cannot yet withstand too much subtle energy. This may even manifest as physical paralysis in the long run. People with heart ailments should not practice Meditation on the Twin Hearts since it may result in severe pranic heart congestion. It is important that people who intend to practice Meditation on the Twin Hearts regularly should also practice self-purification or character building through daily inner reflection. Meditation on the Twin Hearts not only activates the heart chakra and the crown chakra but also the other chakras. Because of this both the positive and negative characteristics of the practitioner be magnified or activated. This can easily be verified by the practitioner himself and through clairvoyant observation.

PROCEDURE

1) Cleansing the etheric body through physical exercise: Do physical exercise for about five minutes. Doing physical exercise has a cleansing and energizing effect on the etheric body. Light grayish matter or used-up prana is expelled from the etheric body when excising. Physical exercises have to be done to minimize possible pranic congestion since this meditation generates a lot of subtle energies in the etheric body.

2) Invocation for divine blessing: Invoking the blessing of one's Spiritual Guides is very important. Each spiritual aspirant has spiritual Guides, whether he or she is consciously aware of them or not he invocation is required for one's protection, help and guidance. Without making the invocation, practicing any advanced meditation technique could be dangerous. You can make your own invocation. I usually use this invocation:

"Father, I humbly invoke Thy divine blessing!
For protection, guidance , help and illumination!
With thanks and in full faith!"

3)Activating the heart chakra-blessing the entire earth with loving-kindness: Press your front heart chakra with your finger for a few seconds. This is to make concentration on the front heart chakra easier. Concentrate on the front heart chakra and bless the earth with loving-kindness. You may improvise your own blessing with loving-kindness. I usually use this blessing:

BLESSING THE EARTH WITH LOVING-KINDNESS

From the Heart of God,
   Let the entire earth be blessed with
   loving-kindness.
   Let the entire earth be blessed with great joy,
   happiness and divine peace.
   Let the entire earth be blessed with
   understanding harmony, goad will and
   with will-to-good. So be it!

From the Heart of Gad,
   Let the hearts of all sentient beings be filled
   with divine love and kindness.
   Let the hearts of all sentient beings filled
   with great joy, happiness and divine peace.
   Let the hearts of all sentient beings filled
   with understanding, harmony, good will and
   will-to-good. With thanks, so be it!

For beginners, this blessing is done only once or twice. Do not overdo this blessing at the start. Some may even feel a slight pranic congestion around the heart area. This is because your etheric body is not sufficiently clean. Apply localized sweeping to remove the congestion.

This blessing should not be done mechanically. You should feel and appreciate the implications in each phrase. You may also use visualization. When blessing the earth with loving-kindness, visualize the aura of the earth as becoming dazzling pink. When blessing the earth with great joy, happiness and peace, visualize people with heavy difficult problems smiling - their hearts filled with joy, faith, hope and peace. Visualize their problems becoming lighter and their faces lightening up. When blessing the earth with harmony, good will and will-to-good, visualize people or nations on the verge of fighting or fighting each other reconciling. Visualize these people putting down their arms and embracing each other. Visualize them being filled with good intentions and filled with the will to carry' out this good intention. This blessing can be directed to a nation or nations, a family or a person or a group of people. Do not direct this blessing on a specific infant or specific children because they might be overwhelmed by the intense energy generated by the meditation.

4) Activating the crown chakra-blessing the earth with loving-kindness: Press the crown with your finger for several seconds to facilitate concentration on the crown chakra and bless the entire earth with loving-kindness. When the crown chakra is fully opened some of you will feel something blooming on top of the head and some will also feel something pressing on the crown. After the crown chakra has been activated, concentrate simultaneously on the crown chakra and the heart chakra, and bless the earth with loving-kindness several times. This will align the heart chakra and the crown chakra, thereby making the blessing much more potent.

5) To achieve illumination-meditation on the light, on the Aum and the gap between the two Aums: Visualize a grain of dazzling white light on the crown or at the center inside the head, and simultaneously mentally utter the mantra, Aum. Concentrate intensely on the point of light, on the Aum and on the gap between the two Aums. When mentally uttering the mantra Aum, you will notice that the Aums are not continuous and that there is a slight gap between two mantras or between two Aums. Do this meditation for five to ten minutes. When the spiritual aspirant can fully concentrate simultaneously on the point of light and on the gap between the two Aums, he or she will experience an "inner explosion of light." The entire being will be filled with light! He be she will have the first glimpse of illumination and the first experience of divine ecstasy! To experience Buddhic consciousness or illumination is to experience and understand what Jesus meant when he said: "If thine

eye be single, thy whole body shall be full of light"
(Luke 11:34). "For behold, the kingdom of heaven is
within you" (Luke 17:21).

For some people, it may take years before
they experience an initial glimpse of illumination or
Buddhic consciousness. Others may take months while
others may take weeks. For the very few, they achieve
initial expansion of consciousness on the first try.
This is usually done with the help from an elder or a
facilitator

When doing this meditation, the aspirant
should be neutral. He or she should not be obsessed
with results or filled with too much expectations.
Otherwise, he or she will be actually meditating on
the expectations or the expected results rather than
on the point of light, the Aum and the gap between
the two Aums.

6) Releasing excess energy: After the end of the
meditation, the excess energy should be released by
blessing the earth with Light, Love and Peace.
Otherwise, the etheric body will become congested
and the visible body will deteriorate in the long run
because of too much energy. Other esoteric schools
release the excess energy by visualizing the chakras
projecting out the excess energy' and the chakras
becoming smaller and dimmer but this approach does
not put the excess energy' into constructive use.

7] Giving thanks: After the end of the meditation,
always give thanks to your spiritual guides for the
divine blessing.

8) Strengthening the visible physical body through
massage and more physical exercises: After the end
of the meditation, massage your body and do physical
exercise for about five minutes. The purpose is to
further cleanse and strengthen the visible body since
more used-up prana is expelled out of the body. This
facilitates the assimilation of the pranic and spiritual
energies, thereby enhancing the beauty and health of
the practitioner. Massaging and exercising after this

meditation also reduces the possibility of pranic congestion or energy getting in certain parts of the body which may lead to illness. You can also gradually cute yourself of some ailments by doing exercises after doing the Meditation on the Twin Hearts, It is very important to exercise after the meditation; otherwise, the visible physical body will inevitably be weakened. Although the etheric body will become very bright and strong, the visible physical body will become weak because it will not be able to withstand the leftover energy generated by the meditation in the long run. You have to experience it yourself to frilly appreciate what I am saying.

Some of you have the tendency not to do physical exercises after this meditation but to continue savoring the blissful state. This tendency should be overcome, otherwise your physical health will deteriorate in the long run.

Sometimes when a spiritual aspirant meditates, he or she may experience unusual physical movements for a limited period of time. This is quite normal since the etheric channels are being cleansed.

The instructions may seem quite long but the meditation is short, simple and very effective! It requires only ten to fifteen minutes excluding the time required for the physical exercises.

There are many degrees of illumination, The art of "intuiting" or direct synthetic knowing" requires constant practice (meditation) for a long duration of time. To be more exact, it requires many incarnations to develop facility in the use of this Buddhic faculty.

Blessing the earth with loving-kindness can be done in group as a form of world service. When done in a group for this purpose, first bless the earth with loving-kindness through the heart chakra, then through the crown chakra, then through both the crown chakra and the heart chakra. Release the excess energy after the end of the meditation. The other parts of the meditation are omitted. The blessing can be directed, not only to the entire earth, but also to a specific nation or group of nations The potency of the blessing is increased many times when done in a group. For example, when the blessing is done by a group of seven, the effect or potency is equal to more than one hundred people doing it separately.

Just as pranic healing can miraculously cure simple and severe ailments, the Meditation on Twin Hearts, when practiced by a large number of people, can also miraculously heal the entire earth . This message is directed to readers with sufficient maturity and he will-to-good.

MEDIATION ON THE TWIN HEARTS

1) Clean the etheric body; do physical exercise for about five minutes.

2) Invoke for divine blessing.

3) Activate the heart chakra, concentrate on it, and bless the entire earth with loving-kindness.

4) Activate the crown chakra, concentrate on it, and bless the entire earth with loving-kindness. Then bless the earth with loving-kindness simultaneously through the crown chakra and the heart chakra.

5) To achieve illumination, concentrate on the point of light, on the Aum, and on the gap between the two Aums.

6) To release excess energy, bless the earth with light, love and peace.

7) Give thanks.

8) To strengthen the visible physical body; massage face and body, and do physical exercise for about five minutes.

Meditation on the Twin Hearts is a very powerful tool in bringing about world peace; therefore, this meditation technique should be disseminated. Permission is granted to all interested persons to reprint, copy, and reproduce the Meditation on the Twin Hearts with proper acknowledgment to both author and publisher. [Choa 1993, 141-149]

In addition to the "Meditation on the Twin Hearts" Choa advises that another good meditation to clean and bring energy to the healer's body is the "Meditation on the White Light". This is another wonderful and fulfilling meditation that should be used by anyone who desire to practice the art of pranic healing. The meditation is as follows:

MEDITATION ON THE WHITE LIGHT

THIS METHOD of general cleansing and energizing is usually called meditation on the white light or meditation on the middle pillar. The middle pillar technique has been used by various oriental and occidental esoteric schools. This technique is divided into parts. The first part deals with general cleansing and energizing. The second part deals with the circulation of prana.

GENERAL CLEANSING AND ENERGIZING

I) Do pranic breathing and simultaneously visualize a ball of intense bright fight above the crown.

2) Visualize a stream of light coming down from the ball to the crown, then gradually down to the feet. Visualize the white light cleansing and energizing all the major chakras, all the important organs, the spine, and the bones in the body.

3) Visualize the white light coming out of the feet and flushing out all the grayish diseased matter Repeat the process three times.

4) Visualize a brilliant ball of light at the bottom of the feet. Draw in earth prana in the form of a stream of fight from this brilliant ball of light. Inhale and draw in the prana through the sole chakras up to the head. Exhale and let the prana sprinkle out of the crown chakra. Repeat this three times.

CIRCULATING PRANA

1) Visualize prana circulating from the bottom of the feet, up to the back of the body, up the head, down to the face, to the front of the body, then to the feet. Circulate prana from back to front three times.

2) Reverse the circulation and circulate prana from front to back. Circulate three times.

3) Circulate prana from left to right three times and from right to left three times. The purpose of circulating prana is to evenly distribute prana throughout the body and to prevent pranic congestion in certain parts of the body.

This meditation can be used daily to improve and maintain your health. It is also used by some esoteric students before engaging in activities that require a lot of prana. You may perform this meditation before healing a large number of people. Once you become proficient in this meditation, you will literally feel your body tingle and will feel a strong current moving within and outside your body.
You may also use the excess prana generated to produce "synthetic ki" or navel ki by concentrating on the navel chakra for about ten minutes. Store the "synthetic ki" in the two secondary navel chakras located two inches below the navel. This is done by simply concentrating on two inches below the navel for about three to five minutes. Pranic breathing should be done simultaneously with the preceding instructions. Each of the secondary navel chakras has a big flexible meridian that is used for storing navel ki. In short, the two secondary navel chakras are warehouses for the "synthetic ki". The two secondary navel chakras are called "ki hai" which means "ocean of ki" because these minor chakras are filled with "synthetic Id." It must be repeated

that "synthetic ki" or navel ki is different from prana. The "synthetic ki" is synthesized by the navel chakra and may appear as milky white, whitish red, golden yellow, and other colors. The "synthetic ki" varies in size and in density. Ordinary people have very little "synthetic ki" compared to spiritual aspirants and practitioners of "ki kung".

It would be advisable for you to learn to meditate on the white light and practice it every day. It makes your bioplasmic body cleaner; brighter and denser thereby making you a better healer. [Choa Kok Sui 1993, 151-153]

REV. DR. WILLIAM J. SCHECK

REIKI HEALING
AN OVERVIEW

THE HEALING TOUCH: In *Reiki the Healing Touch*, William Lee Rand presents the following overview of the ancient art of healing know as REIKI: Rand states that a part of the wisdom of many cultures since ancient times is the knowledge that an unseen energy flows through all living things and is connected directly to the quality of health. The existence of this "life force energy" has been verified by recent scientific experiments, and medical doctors are considering the role it plays in the functioning of the immune system and the healing process. One of these ancient wisdoms is known as ***REIKI*** which is a technique for stress reduction and relaxation that allows everyone to tap into an unlimited supply of "life force energy" to improve health and enhance the quality of life.

It is an amazingly simple technique to learn. The ability to use ***REIKI*** is not taught in the usual sense, but is transferred to the student by the ***REIKI*** Master. Its use is not dependent on ones intellectual capacity or spiritual development and, therefore, is available to everyone.

A treatment feels like a wonderful glowing radiance that flows through you and surrounds you. ***REIKI*** treats the whole person including body, emotions, mind and spirit and creates many beneficial effects including relaxation and feelings of peace, security, and well-being. Many have reported miraculous results. ***REIKI*** is a simple, natural, and safe method of spiritual healing and self-improvement that everyone can use. [Rand 1991, 1-17]

SPIRITUAL WISDOM: The word ***REIKI*** can be divided into Rei which means " Spiritual Wisdom". That is the wisdom that comes from God or the Higher Self. This is the God-Consciousness which is all knowing. It understands each person completely. It knows the cause of all problems and difficulties and knows what to do to heal them.

Rei can be defined as the Higher Intelligence that guides the creation and functioning of the universe. *Rei* is a subtle wisdom that permeates everything, both animate and inanimate. This subtle wisdom guides the evolution of all creation ranging from the unfolding of galaxies to the development of life. On a human level, it is available to help us in times of need and to act as a source of guidance in our lives. Because of its infinite nature, it is all knowing. *Rei* is also called *God* and has many other names depending on the culture that has named it. [Rand 1991, 18]

Whereas, *"Ki"* is the *" The Life Force"*. *Ki* means the same as Chi in Chinese, Prana in Sanskrit and Ti or *Ki* in Hawaiian. It has also been called, odic force, orgone, and bioplasma. It has been given many other names by the various cultures that have been aware of it. It is also called the vital life force or the universal life force. This is the nonphysical energy that animates all living things. As long as something is alive, it has life force circulating through it and surrounding it; when it dies, the life force departs. If your life force is low, or if there is a restriction in its flow, you will be more vulnerable to illness. When it is high, and flowing freely, you are less likely to get sick. Life force plays an important role in everything we do. It animates the body and also is the primary energy of our emotions, thoughts and spiritual life.

Ki is used by martial artists in their physical training and mental development. It is used in meditative breathing exercises called Pranayama, and by the shamans of all cultures for divination, psychic awareness, manifestation and healing. *Ki* is the nonphysical energy used by all healers. *Ki* is present all around us and can be accumulated and guided by the mind. [Rand 1991 18]

SPIRITUALLY GUIDED LIFE FORCE ENERGY:

REIKI can be defined as a non-physical healing energy made up of life force energy that is guided by the Higher Intelligence, or spiritually guided life force energy. This is a functional definition as it closely parallels the experience of those who practice *REIKI* in that *REIKI* energy seems to have an intelligence of its own flowing where it is needed in the client and creating the healing conditions necessary for the individuals needs. It cannot be guided by the mind, therefore it is not limited by the experience or ability of the practitioner. Nether can it be misused as it always creates a healing effect. It must be kept in mind that *REIKI* is not the same as simple life force energy as life force energy by itself can be influenced by the mind and because of this, can create benefit as well as cause problems including ill health.

REIKI is Spiritually Guided Life Force Energy. It is the God-consciousness called Rei that guides the life force called Ki in the practice we call *REIKI*. *REIKI* is a spiritually guided life force energy. This is a meaningful interpretation of the word *REIKI*. It more closely describes the experience most people have of it; *REIKI* guiding itself with its own wisdom, and being unresponsive to the direction of the practitioner.

While *REIKI* is spiritual in nature, it is not a religion. It has no dogma, and there is nothing you must believe in order to learn and use *REIKI*. In fact, *REIKI* is not dependent on belief at all and will work whether you believe in it or not. Because *REIKI* comes from God, many people find that using *REIKI* puts them more in touch with the experience of their religion rather than having only an intellectual concept of it.

While *REIKI* is not a religion, for optimum well being in the light of Eastern medical theory that we are a mind-body-spirit unity, it is necessary to live and act in a way that promotes harmony with others. Dr. Mikao Usui, the founder of the *REIKI* system of natural healing, recommended that one practice certain simple ethical ideals to promote peace and harmony, which are nearly universal across all cultures. [Rand 1991, 19-21]

THE ETHICAL PRINCIPLES OF REIKI:

During a meditation several years after developing *REIKI*, Dr. Usui received the *REIKI IDEALS* [The Ethical Principles of *REIKI*]. The Ideals were given to him to add spiritual balance to his healing work. Their purpose is to help people realize that healing the spirit by consciously deciding to improve oneself is a necessary part of the *REIKI* healing experience. In order for the *REIKI* healing energies to have lasting results, the client must accept responsibility for her or his healing and take an active part in it Therefore, the Usui system of *REIKI* is more than the use of the *REIKI* energy. It must also include an active commitment to improve oneself in order for it to be a complete system. The ideals are both guidelines for living a gracious life and virtues worthy of practice for their inherent value.

Just for Today:
I will let go of anger.
I will let go of worry.
I will give thanks for my many blessings.
I will do my work honestly.
I will be kind to my neighbor and every living being. [Rand 1991, 1-12]

HEALING BY MOVEMENT OF LIFE FORCE ENERGY:

REIKI heals by moving energy or the life force through the body. We are alive because life force is flowing through us. Life force flows within the physical body though pathways called chakras, meridians and nadis. It also flows around us in a field of energy called the aura. Life force nourishes the organs and cells of the body, supporting them in their vital functions. When this flow of life force is disrupted, it causes diminished function in one or more of the organs and tissues of the physical body.

The life force is responsive to thoughts and feelings. It becomes disrupted when we accept, either consciously or unconsciously, negative thoughts or feelings about ourselves. These negative thoughts and feelings attach themselves to the energy field and cause a disruption in the flow of life force. This diminishes the vital function of the organs and cells of the physical body.

REIKI heals by flowing through the affected parts of the energy field and charging them with positive energy. It raises the vibratory level of the energy field in and around the physical body where the negative thoughts and feelings are attached. This causes the negative energy to break apart and fall away. In so doing, *REIKI* clears, straightens and heals the energy pathways, thus allowing the life force to flow in a healthy and natural way.

CHANNELED HEALING: Because *REIKI* is guided by the God-consciousness, it can never do harm. It always knows what a person needs and will adjust itself to create the effect that is appropriate for them. One never need worry about whether to give *REIKI* or not. It is always helpful. In addition, because the practitioner does not direct the healing and does not decide what to work on, or what to heal, the practitioner is not in danger of taking on the karma of the client. Because the practitioner is not doing the healing, it is also much easier for the ego to stay out of the way and allow the presence of God to clearly shine through.

Because it is a *channeled healing*, the *REIKI* practitioner's energies are never depleted. In fact, the *REIKI* consciousness considers both practitioner and client to be in need of healing, so both receive treatment. Because of this, giving a treatment always increases one's energy and leaves one surrounded with loving feelings of well-being. [Rand 1991, 22 - 28]

REIKI TREATMENT METHODOLOGY: The recommended methodology for giving a *REIKI* treatment is:

1] Clear the energy in the room by burring sage or essential oils.

2] Explain the *REIKI* process to your client.

3] Ask you client to remove jewelry and quartz watches to eliminate potential interference in the flow of *REIKI* energy or its harmonizing effect.

4] Wash your hands and make sure that the client is comfortable.

5] Before starting the treatment ask the client to be mediate with the thought of being thankful for the healing which will come to him/her.

6] Perform the main invocation according to hermetic law is *"as above so below"*. By setting the ego to one side and making contact with the true Self, you open yourself to greater receptivity of *REIKI.*

5] Scan your client's body and aura that is look for disease in the physical body as manifested in the client's aura.

6] Establish a gentile psychic contact with the client. Mediate on the *REIKI* energies, and on the conscious of *REIKI* allowing your conscious to become one with the *REIKI* consciousness. Also, make you mind one with the client's mind in order to project positive thoughts to the client such as "I know I am healed, I known I am solving my problems, or affirmations you and your client have formulated.

7] End the *REIKI* treatment by sealing the client's energy field and your own with divine love and wisdom and by smoothing the aura of the client from head to foot. [Lubeck 1996, 40] [Rand 1991, 44-45]

One can create the *REIKI* energy flowing in oneself simply by stating the word *REIKI*. *REIKI* is always ready to flow and it will do so whenever you want it! It is not necessary to meditate to cause *REIKI* to flow. Just placing your hand on a client to do a healing will cause the *REIKI* energy to flow. *REIKI* comes out of love, kindness and compassion and will automatically flow to those areas of you clients' body which require a healing. *REIKI* healing is self-directing and creates a healing miracle in your client and yourself. You can use *REIKI* to heal yourself as well as your client. While you are doing *REIKI,* you will feel it flow your body into client. The flow of *REIKI* in your body will create feelings of joy, love, well-being, security, up-liftment, unlimited potential, freedom, creativity, beauty, balance, harmony and other positive states. Allow these feelings to become your feelings and transfer them to your client. As you allow *REIKI* to flow in your body into your client's body both you and your patient will receive a deep healing. [Rand 1991, 40-41]

RADIATORY HEALING
BIOMAGNETISM

According to Franz Bardon in his book *Initiation Into Hermetics,* miracle healings are created through the use of *Vital Force Energies* and biomagnetism. *Vital Force Energy* is obtained by breathing in a regular fashion and bring the energy into your body from the *Universe*. As you breath in, you store the energy in your body and keep the energy in your body when you breath out. You fill your body with energy each time that you breath in. Also, you can bring *Vital Force Energy* into you body through the pores into your skin. You mentally open the pores in your skin and suck the energies into your pores filling up your body with this energy. You can also return this *Vital Force Energy* to the universe by breathing it out. This energy can be use to heal the sick by radiating it to them. [Bardon 1993, 84-85]

However, in order to make the most effective use of this *Vital Force Energy*, the healer must have an understanding of the laws of biomagnetism that is how to prevent the *Vital Force Energy* which you radiate for a healing from dissolving and mingling with other vibrations and in effect fading away over time. The *Vital Force* accepts not only a thought or a feeling. but also involves time-ideas. Therefore, when impregnating desires with the aid of vital energy, remember time and space. It is important to consider the following rules:

> *1] Working in the akasha-principle is timeless and spaceless.*
> *2] In the metal sphere, you operate with time.*
> *3] In the astral sphere, you work with space [shape, colour].*
> *4] In the material world, you work with time and space simultaneously.[Bardon 1993, 88]*

HEALING MAGNETISM
IMAGINATION AND WILLPOWER:

Healing magnetism can be used to treat a sick person by magnetic strokes, by putting hands on, or at distance through the use of imagination and will-power. However, to do so, the healer must exactly observe the law of time if he desires to be successful. The healer with the aid of imagination makes his *Vital Force* flow out of his body for example from his hands into the sick person. The patient is healed only when the healer has been psychically open, that he has accomplished a dynamic accumulation of *Vital Force* in his own body and emits light-rays of

Vital Force. The healer must always maintain his imagination combined with the desire concentration, wishing that the patient be better and better, hour by hour, from day to day.

2. FINDINGS:

THE STEAMING FORTH OF RADIANT ENERGY: Before begin a treatment, the healer must fill his body with the *Vital Force Energy* as described in the aforesaid. This should produce a radiance around the healer's body causing his body to light up like the sun. The healer does not have to touch the patient or be near the patient to transfer this healing energy to the patient. The healer imagines that the radiant energy surrounding him will stream forth into the patient's body penetrating and illumining all the pores of the sick person. Then, the healer lets or commands his will-power to bring about the recovery of the patient. When using this method the healer's radiant energy which he transferred to the patient does not diminish, but keeps on lighting up in the same manner as before because the *Vital Power* accumulated in the body of the healer renews itself automatically. Consequently, a healer can treat hundreds of patients without running his mental strength or his nerves. The aforesaid is the use of magnetism for treatment of patients over time and space; and if the healer works this treatment in the akasha principle of timelessness and spacelessness, he can effect cures thousands of miles away from the patient. Bardon stated " high adepts and Saints who have trained their imaginations to such a perfection that all their imageries are realized immediately in all planes, do not need methods any more. Such people have only to express any kind of desire and it will be realized in the very same moment." [Bardon 1993, 89-94].

CHAPTER IV
DISCUSSION

At various times while we are on our earth walk, we are in need of a miracle. We suffer from pain in our body, mind, soul and spirit. Miracles can relieve that pain and suffering and makes us one with God again. Often times the miracle that we are seeking is to remove pain and suffering from our physical body. Sometimes, we have so much physical pain and suffering that we cry out to God for help for a miracle to relieve it, make it go away, and make us whole again. Through our studies, we have learned that there are many ways to relieve pain and suffering from our bodies, minds, souls and spirits. The catalysis for removing this pain is using the force of God's energies to intercede on our behalf to enter into our bodies, minds, soul and spirits to remove the energies which are causing us and others our pain and suffering.

The charismatics go directly to God in prayer and ask for a miracle. They ask for God to intercede on their behalf and create the miracle of energy which removes the pain and suffering. Faith, prayer, and a belief that God will perform a miracle is what creates the miracle. The knowning-ness, that God is loving, kind and supernatural and can cause energy to move through time and space to create a healing, is all that is need. This is a direct call to God to intercede on one's behalf or on the behalf of another to bring healing energies to us to remove our pain and suffering. This energy knows no boundaries of time or space and is infinite in nature. This is the God-Conscious Energy which we can evoke for ourselves and others by praying to God for a miracle, by invoking this energy through prayer. This is the beautiful golden-white healing energy of God that comes to us for the asking for God always answers our prayers *if we have faith*. This energy can be used for the laying-on-hand, for financial intervention, for whatever miracle one desires. It is ours for the asking, but most of us do not known how to ask, for we ignore the miracle powers of God through prayer and intercession. For all we have to say is: ***God let your miracle energy enter me and heal me and let me use that energy to heal others. Amen!***

When we questions our mind what is this energy that brings healing? Often, we need a scientific explanation! That is an explanation which can be explained in both the physical and metaphysical world. Such an explanation is given by the concepts of Spirit Energy which is sound and light, divine in nature, and comes to us through meditation. All creatures and things in the cosmos are created in, from, and through waves of sound and light. Sound and light waves result in electromagnet currents. Electromagnetic current radiate to all directions of space and beyond. Part of electromagnetic current is visible light. The light, we can see with the physical organ of sight. We soon realize every substance in the universe is made of light and the universe is a hologram of which we are a part and God is the whole. We are co-creators with God because we are a part of the God-Hologram. This means at any time we can call upon the energy within us and God to create a healing. We can activate this God-Hologram Energy of Divine Light and Sound vibrations to heal us and others. Through this Hologram, we can tape into higher levels of God-Consciousness and create healings in our bodies, minds, souls and spirits.

As we learn more about energy, we realize consciousness is a form of energy. The higher states of consciousness can be used to bring energy to a specific location. This localized energy can be used for healing. *This is calling upon the God-Consciousness as form of energy to channel through us and to use this energy for healing.* Our illness may be a symbolic reflection of our own internal states of emotional unrest, spiritual blockage, and dis-ease. Our subtle energetic components that is chakras and meridian systems, translate our emotional and spiritual difficulties into physiological weaknesses which may eventual result in localized systems breakdown in the physical body that is disease. When disease occurs, it is a sign that we are constricting the natural flow of creative consciousness and subtle life energies through our multi-dimensional body/mind/spirit complex. It is an indicator that something has going wrong with the system and the system must be re-balanced if lasting health is to be obtained. Many of the basic emotions/spiritual issues which we are trying to work through are reflected in key lesions of the chakras. These chakras issues relate to grounding, sexuality, personal power, love, will, creative expression, inner vision, and spiritual seeking. When there is a blockage in working through one of these key life issues, it can result in the blockage of the flow of energy in the corresponding chakra to the aforesaid issues. This can constrict the flow of life energy to the associated body organ system[s]. The blockage can express itself in illness both mental and physical. [Gerber 1998, 464, 500 & 501].

This divine energy which we can call upon moves faster than the speed of light. This is the negatively entropic characteristic of the subtle life energies, that is the etheric, astral, mental and causal bodies. In addition, the negative space/time matter is primary magnetic in nature. The energetic fields of healers is negative/space substance, or magneto-electric energy. In that, they demonstrate certain qualitative similarities to magnetic fields. Also, they have negative entropic properties, that is the ability to reassemble disordered molecules such as enzymes. [Gerber 1988, 145-149]

This is demonstrated through the laying-on-of hands healing which is an exchanged between healers and patient of a subtle life-energy of magnetic nature during the land-on-hands. The healing energy is negatively entropic in nature. It caused systems to become more ordered. Research demonstrated that healer's energies can increase hemoglobin levels in patients similar to the way they increase chlorophyll content in healer-treated plants. People can be trained to do healing, that is healing is an innate human potential and it can be a learned skill.

The laying-on-hands healing is magnetic healing. It is works at the physical-etheric levels of re-balancing. It is performed with the healer's hands in close proximity to the patient. Spiritual healers usually work with many levels of mind and spirit as well at the level of the body. It is higher dimensional energy which transcends all limitations of time and space by virtue of the fact that levels from etheric and higher energies are in the domain of negative space/time. As such the energies working at these levels move in dimensions which are outside the usual reference of ordinary [or positive] space/time to which the conscious mind is limited in its perception. Additionally, the frequency at which spiritual healing takes place often extend to the same levels at which the Higher-Self exist and operates. That is we become co-creators with God in the God-Hologram of creation and healing.

As was stated early in this thesis, Panic healing, which is defined as the ancient science and art of healing which utilizes prana, ki or vital energy to heal the whole physical body, mind, soul and spirit, is a very important form of hands-on-healing. Pranic healing involves the manipulation of ki and bioplasmic matter of the patient's body. It has also been called psychic healing, magnetic healing, faith healing, ki healing, vitalic healing and the laying on of hands. [Choa 1990, 1] Prana or ki is the vital energy of life force that keeps the body health and alive. It is also know as the breath of life. *Miraculous healings* occur when the healer projects Prana, vital energy, or the breath of life to the patient thereby healing the patient. The major sources of prana are air, sun, water and earth.

In *The Essene of the Gospel of Peace,* we learn that Jesus the Christ was very knowledgeable of *Prana Healing* and used it to create *miracles*. Jesus was a Shaman who used the elements of forces of Air, Fire [Sunlight], Water, and Earth. All the energies of all the worlds spin like wheels on the Shaman's path. The upper world of the sky journeys, the lower worlds of the earth journeys and the middle world of humankind all connect on the path of the Shaman. All worlds spin and vibrate for the Shaman. The Shaman rides the wheel of each world to feel its vibration and direct power. This is the wisdom of the Shaman. The Shaman must experience the worlds of the riding wheels of vibrations. *This will bring the attunements with the deep shamanic energies of nature.* The Shaman remains rooted in personal connection to the earth by staying centered and balance in the midst of the chaos of spinning wheels of energy and vibration. A Shaman is able to reach into the spirit from the connection with the Earth. "In this way, the *Shaman becomes channel between the energies of the earth and Nature and the energies of Spirit.* Like a living tree, the Shaman is rooted deep in the earth, reaching and growing into Spirit. The Shaman is an Earth connection; the Shaman is connect to Spirit." - God. [Wolfe 1997, xiii]

Jesus was one of the greatest healers of all times. The energies which flowed from him cured the body, mind, soul, and spirit. Jesus stated that there was no mystery to being a healer like him. Everyone can heal if they have faith and believe in God that God can create miracles. We get most of our vital energy from the air we breath. For "Then the Lord God formed man out of the dust of the ground and breathed into his nostrils the breath of life, and man became a living being. [The Bible, Genesis 2:7]

Pranic healing is energy healing. Energy is brought into the healers body, mind. soul, and spirit through mediation and breathing exercisers. The energy is drawn from the air, water, earth and living things such as trees. This energy is concentrated in the healer and released through the chakras in the healer's hand. The energy is used to balance the patient's chokers and remove negative energies from the patient's body, mind, soul and spirit. These negative energies are found in the chakras found in the patient's physical body, etheric, mind and causal bodies [that is the patients' aura]. The negative energies are removed from the patient by the healer and then the healer fills the patient's chakras with healing energy such as a golden white light energy. [Choa 1990, 39 -49]

In addition, we learned that the esoteric healer acts as a catalyst to healing by moving energy in, out and through the chakras which affects the secretion of hormones which directly affect the healing process in the human body. In chemistry a catalyst is defined as a substance that remains unchanged while increasing the rate of reaction between other substances. For instances, enzymes act as catalysts in the digestion of food, enabling chemical changes to take place in their presence. Although we must heal ourselves, the healing process can be facilitated by the catalytic presence of an esoteric healer. [Lansdowne 1986, 12]

There are numerous ways of bring this healing energy to the healer and his client. Two of the most wonderful methods for bring this energy to the healer which were discussed in this study are the Meditations on the Twin Hearts and the White Light. These meditations bring us in touch with the *life force energy* or the *God-Consciousness,* can be made to radiate within us, and from us to create a healing in ourselves and others.

REIKI is another form of energy healing discussed in this study. REIKI is a non-physical healing energy made up of life force energy that is guided by the Higher Intelligence, or spiritually guided life force energy. REIKI heals by flowing through the affected parts of the energy field and charging them with positive energy. It raises the vibratory level of the energy field in and around the physical body where the negative thoughts and feelings are attached. This causes the negative energy to break apart and fall away. In so doing, REIKI clears, straightens and heals the energy pathways, thus allowing the life force to flow in a healthy and natural way.

Because REIKI is guided by the God-consciousness, that is it is channeled healing. It can never do harm! It always knows what a person needs and will adjust itself to create the effect that is appropriate for them. One never need worry about whether to give REIKI or not. It is always helpful. In addition, because the practitioner does not direct the healing and does not decide what to work on, or what to heal, the practitioner is not in danger of taking on the karma of the client. Because the practitioner is not doing the healing, it is also much easier for the ego to stay out of the way and allow the presence of God to clearly shine through. Because it is a channeled healing, the REIKI practitioner's energies are never depleted. In fact, the REIKI consciousness considers both practitioner and client to be in need of healing, so both receive treatment. Because of this, giving a treatment always increases one's energy and leaves one surrounded with loving feelings of well-being. [Rand 1991, 22 - 28]

From Franz Bardon [Bardon 1993, 84-85] who studied the hermetics traditions of ancient Egypt, we discovered that miracle healings are created through the use of *Vital Force Energies* and biomagnetism. *Vital Force Energy* is obtained by breathing in a regular fashion and bring the energy into your body from the *Universe.* As you breath in, you store the energy in your body and keep the energy in your body when you breath out. You fill your body with energy each time that you breath in. Also, you can bring *Vital Force Energy* into you body through the pores into your skin. You mentally open the pores in your skin and. suck the energies into your pores filling up your body with this energy. You can also return this *Vital Force Energy* to the universe by breathing it out. This energy can be use to heal the sick by radiating it to them via the hands using imagination and will-power and thought projections for distant healings.

CHAPTER V
SUMMARY AND CONCLUSION

All of the aforesaid sources of healing come from the spirit, from the God-Consciousness and are channeled to us. We are CO-CREATORS with GOD, the Great Mystery, the Great Spirit. We and God are one when we channel this energy to heal ourselves and others. We are one with the Great Spirit of loving-kindness and wisdom.

Although we seek an understanding of this ***SPIRIT ENERGY*** that heals, there is know understanding of it for it ***just is*** and heals if we call upon it for the miracle of healing, for this is the myth and the magic of the SPIRIT!

> *Let us call Spirit pure energy - but it is known to us only as polarized energy.*

> *Let us call God consciousness - but it is known to us only through complementation.*

> *Let us call the Original Scission the first act of becoming - but it is known to us only as separation. [Lamy 1994, 13]*

> *The great mystery is the passage from invisible into the visible, to be realized by the Power which forms the incomprehensible One call forth in the many [Lamy 1994, 8]*

To create this ***Spirit Energy*** and attune ourselves to it, we must understand the four centers of instruction that is:

> *1] How do we describe the indescribable? 2] How do we show the unshowable? 3] How do we express the unutterable? 4] How do we seize the ungraspable instant? Before there was any opposition, any yes and no, positive and negative; before there was complementarity, high and low, light and shadow; before there was the presence and the absence, of life or death, heaven or earth: there was but one incomprehensible Power ,.... the indefinable cosmic*

sea, the infinite source of the Universe outside the notion of Space and Time." [Lamy 1994, 8]

This is the original *Unity*, the *Spirit Energy* which we call upon and channel to create the miracle of healing of the body, mind, soul and spirit. This is God and we are co-creators with God in everything that we do.

We can evoke this Spirit Energy [Life Force Energy] by asking God to direct it to us. *It is ours for the asking.* Elaborate rituals are not required, just an opening of ones conscious to God and with our imagination and will-power direct the *Spirit Energy* to heal ourselves, others and create the miracles we desire. We can open our consciousness to God through thought, imagination and well-power which will bring the· life force energy [*Spirit Energy*] to us and direct it to ourselves and others to create miracles.

The biggest miracle of all is that this *Spirit Energy* is ours for the asking for it *just is* for our use to heal ourselves and others in body, mind, soul and spirit. God's desire is for us to be whole and one with God. God does not exist in pain and suffering. God never intended us to exist in pain and suffering. We are co-creators with God. We can call upon *God's Spirit Energy* to create our miracles, make us whole, and one with God.

BOOK 3
POEMS

WE HAVE A PLACE

We all have a place,
a place
in our hearts
where
we go to be love.

A place of comfort and joy,
a place that makes us feel good,
and brings us happiness.

This place is in our hearts and souls,
is a place of oneness with ourselves,
with love and God.

Close your eyes
and go into your heart
and you will find you,
GOD,
and
LOVE.

Now close your eyes,
and you are there
in peace and love.

And so it is.

Amen

w.j. scheck
21 feb 2000
santa ana

GLORIOUS TODAY

Oh! Glorious today,
      you are so
      wonderful true.

You are
      what is now,
      and
      ever will be.

You are
      a light
      in the void,
      and
      nothingness
      made real.

For today,
      this moment
      is
      all there is,
      for today
      is our only time,
      are only essence.

For today
      is us
      our souls,
      our essence
      and are bliss.

w.j. scheck
21 feb 2000
santa ana

MY LOVE

To know me now,
       yes,
       and
       only now
       has a wonderful thought
       for I am you,
       all of you,
       and I am love.

Yes, good sweet tender love
       that is waiting
       for you
       at the end of time,
       I am
       the essence
       of love.

And to know
       me now
       is to look
       into your heart
       and
       see rays of love
       shining like the sun.

And to feel
       the warm rays
       all around you.

Encompassing you
       and love
       that will make
       you know me now.

My love.

w.j. scheck
21 feb 2000
santa ana

A PART OF THIS BEAUTY

I am a stranger here
        and so are you
        we are strangers in this strange land,
        but we are here to be a part of the it
        for a short period of our essence.

We are here to flow
        with the beauty of this land
        and to take in the sunrises and sunsets,
        the blue skies and the snow covered mountains,
        the green grass and plowed fields.

We are here
        to be a part of this beauty, and to remember it for all of our
        essence
        to hold it the dearly in our hearts.

We are here in this strange land
        to find our essence
        with the joy of living and love,
        and to thank God
        for this short period of our essence
        to live in this beauty and love.

AMEN!

w.j. scheck
21 feb 2000
santa ana

A PLACE CALLED GLORY, A PLACE CALLED GOD

There once was a place not far from here
      a place called glory,
      a place called love,
      a place where our essence meets our love,
      and God says hello.

How do I know,
      because I've been there,
      in my dreams,
      in my heart,
      and in my soul,
      this place is dear to me,
      because it is me,
      my essence,
      all that there is of me,
      and all that there is of you,
      this place is a place in the sun,
      a place where the clouds the meet the sky,

This place is my home,
      my very precious home,
      where I come from,
      were life was always good for me,
      and where I was always one with God, a
      place where I walked with God.

Don't you have a place like
      this for yourself,
      where you speak to God
      and God speaks to you?

If you could only see God in your heart,
      then you will know the wonder
      of being one with God.

If you could only see me now,
      then you would see the tears of joy
      running down my face,
      the joy in my heart,

the joy in my soul,
the joy in my essence,
the joy in my love,
the joy in me, you, us, and God.

When my time comes to leave this earth,
I will leave with joy and happiness
in knowing
that I have a wonderful opportunity
to be here with all of you,
yes.
and to find God in all of you
and in everything
that is a apart of this dimension called earth,
as I leave I will say goodbye to all of your
with joy in my heart
and with all of my love that I have,
that I received from the you and from God.

As I a journey on,
I give thanks for all I experienced
for all that has made me what I am
and what has happened to me,
yes,
I give thanks for all
that has happened.

When I enter that place in the sky,
to be one with the Great Mystery,
called Love,
called Wonderful,
called Beautiful,
called Hope,
called Faith,
called God!

I will be there forever
and I will always be with God,
and it is so
and it is true
and it always will be
and so it is!.

Look at me,
        look into my essence,
        look into my soul,
        look into me,
        you will see The All,
        you will see the Great Mystery,
        you will see so much and be so amazed
        at what you know,
        yes see you are apart of God,
        and you cannot deny it,
        forever more!

And you will be in a place
        not far from here
        a place called glory,
        a place called love,
        a place where our essence meets our love,
        and where God says hello.

A place called GLORY, a place called GOD!

w.j. scheck
santa ana
30 july 2000

ANOTHER TIME

Another time,
>I could have been here

Another time,
>I could have been here,
>but God has given me
>no more time,
>but a few moments
>that are now gone.

Another time,
>I could have been here
>to love you,
>but God has given me
>no more time,
>and now my moments
>are gone.

Another time,
>we could have made sweet love,
>but God has given me
>no more time
>to make sweet love
>to you.

Another time,
>we could have dance all night,
>but God has given me
>no more time to dance
>with you.

Another time,
>we could have spent
>the rest of our lives together,
>but God has given me more moments
>to be here.

So in the few moments that I have,
> I am going to say good bye
> with love, and thank God
> for the time
> that I have had with you

w.j. scheck
21 feb 2000
santa ana

BUSINESSMAN

I'm your businessman,
Baby, Baby
yea,
I sure am your sweet lover man.

Yea, Baby, Baby,
I am your businessman,
and I am here
Baby, Baby
to give you the business
of love straight
from my heart to yours.

For I am your businessman,
Baby, Baby,
I sure am,
you lover man.

w.j. scheck
blues cafe, long beach, ca
29 mar 1999

CALL IT LOVE

Some call it love,
>   love that last forever,
>   some call you,
>   my Dear Sweet Love,
>   my lover for all of time.

Some call it essence of love,
>   essence of you
>   that will
>   just always be.

Some say love,
>   your love
>   and my love
>   is the kind of love
>   that last forever,
>   and just will be.

Some say hello,
>   I love you,
>   and I do,
>   I just love you forever,
>   my Dear Sweet Love.

·And some say,
>   we are one,
>   one love
>   forever more.

Yes,
>   some call it love,
>   love that last forever,
>   some call you,
>   my Dear Sweet Love,
>   my love
>   for all of time.

w.j. scheck
santa ana
15 mar 2000

DREAM LOVE

Let me dream the words of the Great Spirit,
      let me hear the words in my dreams,
      let the words of love be a part me,
      of the dream,
      for in my heart
      I feel words and dream,
      many dreams of love.

Love that touches my soul,
      my essence,
      my me,
      love that is always a part of me,
      love that can change the world,
      love that is like a shining sun
      that radiates love and compassion to the world
      and love that is of God,
      of our of essence,
      of our being and always with us
      when we walk our earth journey
      and that carries us to the stars.

Love that is of us,
      love
      that is Gods word and a dream
      that was always in our essence

Love that makes us
      love,
      love that brings God to us
      and us to God.

w.j. scheck
santa ana
31 dec 1998

IF YOU EVER MAKE A LOVE SONG

If you ever make a love song for me,
        tell me about the stars
        and you and me.

And your sweet kisses,
        and a soft touches on my lips.

Sing how much you love me
        when the sun shines on my face,
        and we awaken in the morning.

Sing how much you love me
        when we kiss in the morning and hold each other,
        and tell me you will love me for all time.

And always loved me.

And when you make that love song,
        sing it from your heart,
        with all your heart,
        and always sing a song of love
        for me
        for all of time.

w.j. scheck
santa ana
1 august 1998

PASSING

Time

        is a passing,
        time
        that always is
        and will always be a way
        into your heart,
        a key
        that
        opens the door
        to pure
        true love
        that
        always will
        be.

Love

        is
        that time
        in our hearts
        that last forever,
        and just always there
        to make
        our hearts warm,
        and
        to bring us closer
        and
        closer together
        for all time.

Yes,

        time is
        always passing
        into
        our hearts
        and
        our love
        is there
        for
        all
        of
        time!

w.j. scheck
21 august 1999
santa ana

LIVING IN THE SOUL OF GOD

The world around us
      is a miracle
      it is God's way
      of allowing us to know God.

All the beauty we see and feel
      is God's spirit and soul
      and we are a part of it.

The sun, moon, stars, water, wind, rain, snow, flowers, rocks, the good
earth
      that gives us life and God providing for us,
      and God's way of letting us know God

When we pass through the dimensions of earth,
      we already living in the soul of God,

And we are a part of God's love and beauty.

w.j. scheck
santa ana
27 jun 2000

RED MOUNTAIN GOD

Oh!
> I am but a vision of insanity,
> on a long walk to my sanity.

Who am I?
> but an illusion of the Red Mountain.

Oh!
> Red Mountain,
> why have you brought me to you?

Oh!
> why have you brought me to your feet?

Red Mountain who am I but a vision of insanity,
> an illusion of disbelief,
> why have you brought me to you?

Why, am I,
> why, am I,
> and where am I?

Oh!
> Red Mountain God
> who are you
> to make me sane,
> can't I be me,
> just me,
> just insane me,
> why do you bring me
> to you?

What do you want of me?
> I am but a vision of nothingness,
> I am insane.

Why do you want me?
> Oh! Red Mountain God!

Why?
Why?

When I am nothing, but insane!
        you should beckon me in my sane days,
        when I was something
        when I was a Sun-God
        when my rays were bright
        and I was the light,
        when I was all of powerful.

But, now you want me,
        and I am in insane,
        I am nothing,
        I am the Great Nothingness,
        and yet Red Mountain you want me!

Why?

Why?

When I have nothing , but my nothingness

Yet!

Red Mountain God,
        you want me to ascend the mountain
        to glory
        to be one with you
        in my insanity.

Why is this,
        what do you want of me?
        For, I am nothing in my nothingness!

Why is this,
        what do you want of me?
        For, I am nothing in my nothingness!

And yet
        you want me,
        to climb the mountain

to be a part of your glory.
Now, I am with you,
    and I am humbled.
    Why is this?
    Oh! Red Mountain God!
    Who are you?
    Who are you
    that you want me
    and my insane nothingness?
    Are you me, are you god?

Yes, you must be!

Yes, you must be!
    And I am you and God!
    You brought me to your feet
    and you gave me your glory
    even when I was nothing and insane
    and I became apart of you.
    I am humbled!

And thankful,
    for your love and glory,
    and the Red Mountain in my vision,
    in my soul,
    that gave me you and God!

w.j. scheck
santa ana
7 jul 2000

SEE ME NOW

If you can only see me now,
          see the tears in my heart,
          and my crying for you,
          if you can only see the tears in my heart,
          than you would truly know,
          how much I miss you,
          when you are not here with me,
          if you only knew how hard my life is without you,
          than you would come running back to me.

And put your arms around me,
          and say it will all be OK
          for I truly love you with all my heart
          and will until the end of time,
          you must know how much I miss you
          and always will with all my heart
          with all of my tears
          I will always miss you
          until the end of time
          I will cry for you cry, cry
          crying with all my heart
          until you are in my arms again
          I will cry forever and ever
          until you put your arms around me again!

Yes, if you could only see me now,
          you would know I am in the pain without you,
          and I will always be in sorrow
          until you put your arms around me again,
          and tell me that I am your only love for all of time.

Please tell me,
          that you will be home soon
          and we will be in love again,
          and our love will always be true and pure,
          until the end of time,
          don't forsake me,
          please don't leave me,
          please don't leave the for I will die.

w.j. scheck
santa ana
23 jul 2000

SO FIND

You were only sixteen ,
> but you're my sweet little thing,
> that I love,
> and you were so fine.

I would like to tell you ,
> you were that love of mine,
> because you were so fine,
> so sweet
> and you were pretty and so fine.

You were my sweetheart
> of the lovely,
> sweet kind.

w.j. scheck
Blues Cafe
Long Beach, California
14 August 1999

TRUE

One more moment,
     just
     one more moment
     and baby
     our love
     will be
     forever
     true.

Yes,
     just
     one more moment
     with you
     and our kisses
     will
     will
     last forever
     and our love
     will be forever
     true.

Kiss me one more time
     and tell me
     you love me
     and our love
     will be forever
     true.

One more moment
     and our love
     will forever be
     true.

w.j. scheck
Blues Cafe,
Long Beach California
14 August 1999

STAR PEOPLE

They come,
> here,
> in glory,
> from the stars,
> and become one
> with you.

But, you reject them,
> you reject their love
> and they cry
> in their souls for you.

For you reject their love,
> they left,
> and you became more primitive,
> and war like
> and you hated yourselves,
> and you remembered the loss love
> of the stair people, and you cried.

You still see the miracles
> they created
> and you wonder how was it down.

Then you created a revenge will god
> and use this god to destroy each other
> In the name of god.
> but in reality
> in the name of man.

And you spend a great deal of your time
> looking at the stars, wondering what happened,
> and waiting.

Waiting!

Waiting!

For the star people to return,

for God
to return to you,
you who abandoned God>

And God will return
        until you open your hearts to love,
        and the star people will return
        and all will be good again.

w.j. scheck
santa ana
24 Jul 2000

GOD HIS TRUTH / LOVE

Life equals truth,
> and truth equals belief
> and believing equals you,
> God,
> love,
> and
> Life Energy.

You are what you believe,
> and what you believe
> is what you create.

When you
> believe in love,
> you co-create love
> with God.

God is your truth,
> your love,
> your belief,
> and
> becomes
> your reality,
> your essence
> and you.

God is in you,
> and God is your love,
> you are love
> and joy
> apart of god.

This is true,
> this is the truth,
> and this is God,
> your God
> who loves you
> and gives you joy and peace
> and always love.

And so it is!

w.j. scheck

santa ana

26 july 2000

REV. DR. WILLIAM J. SCHECK

A PART OF ME

There is apart of me,
      that says hello to God,
      there is apart of me
      that says love,
      apart that cries out love, love,
      apart that hold my essence up to God.

There is apart in me
      that says all day long
      I want to be with you
      my love
      my God.

.Their is apart of me that knows no boundaries
      apart that opens
      my heart totally to God.

There is a part of the me
      that cries out from deep inside my essence
      love, love, love
      I love you with all my heart,
      God I love you.

There is a knowing inside me
      that fills me with joy of God,
      a joy
      that lasted for be eternity,
      a joy
      that is always with me.

Oh!

My god
      you have been so wonderful to me,
      you have given me joy, love, peace,
      the essence of your love of you,
      you have given me
      all of these things.

And,

        I will always be with you
        forever and ever in all my days
        which I will spend in contemplate of you,
        of the joy, peace, and happiness
        that you have given me,
        I will spent my life in love,
        a love that you have given to me ,
        and I will always be in love with you ,
        I will always love you
        and I will let your love penetrate me
        all days of my life,
        all of my essence,
        all my soul,
        and I will always wanted you to know
        your our my savior,
        my Love,
        my God,
        my purpose
        for being here on earth

Thank you God

        for the joy
        you have brought me
        thank you for the wind,
        the stars,
        the trees,
        the ocean, the sun
        everything you have given me
        for all love
        you have made apart of me,
        thank you very much
        thank you
        from the depth of my heart
        and
        thank you with all the joy.
        I can give you
        and all my love.

w.j. scheck
santa ana
29 july 2000

TIME IS

Time is a passing,
        time that always
        is
        and will always be
        a way
        into your heart,
        a key
        that opens the door
        to pure true love
        that always will
        be.

Love is
        that time in our hearts
        that last forever,
        and just always there
        to make our heart warm,
        and to bring us closer
        and closer together for all time.

Yes, time is
        always passing
        into our hearts
        and our love
        is there
        for all of time!

Yes, our love and time
        are for all of time!

w.j. scheck
santa ana
18 april 1999

TIME FOR IT

We had a time for it,
          yes we did,
          we had time for love,
          that is forever and a day.

Then, we got caught up in it,
          and forgot the time of day,
          forgot the love of our moment.

What doesn't mean?

When we had it all,
          love,
          but,
          we get caught up in it,
          and lost the moment of our love.

Then, some say
          that in just the way it is.

And, there is no more love moments.

But, that cannot be for
          there is always another
          moment in the day.

w.j. scheck
san juan cap.
at the oaks
7 august 1999

SHARE YOUR LIFE WITH GOD

There is but one life,
        and it is your life,
        to live and share
        with THE ALL
        WITH GOD.

You are the one
        who must open your heart
        to GOD,
        because God
        is the one
        who loves you
        and is always
        open
        to you.

Do not reject God,
        for in doing so
        you reject yourself,
        you reject your love
        of yourself
        for God is love
        your love.

And love is God,
        open yourself
        to love
        of yourself
        and
        open yourself
        to God. to

And in so doing
        you
        will share
        your life
        with God.

Amen!

I SAY LOVE

So they say many,
    many things,
    but who are they,
    for they are not me.

I say love,
    love is what I say
    it is all about.

But many people
    do not know much about love,

Because their hearts are closed
    and
    I say
    open your hearts
    for here

I am

    in your essence,
    in your soul
    and yes

I am

    Love.

You must
    know me
    for

I am

    the one
    who creates
    loving- kindness
    in you
    and gives
    you love.

I am

the one
who makes you
soft and tender
and gives you
sweet kindness.

I am

your essence.

I am

the love and lover.

I am

what you call God.

I am

you
in the essence
of LOVE!

w.j. scheck
22 jul 2000
santa ana

WATERFALL

There is a waterfall
   in my dreams,
   a mystery
   which flows
   down
   on me.

A mystery of flowing love
   encompassing
   me
   which
   showers me
   with love,
   love that encompasses
   me.

Waterfall of my dreams
   with love
   falling down on you and me,
   water that cleans our souls
   and makes our kisses cool and sweet,
   kisses that last for a million years,
   and
   love like this waterfall,
   flowing to our hearts.

Love of my dreams.

w.j. scheck
santa ana
22 july 2000

WHERE ARE YOU GOING?

Where are you going,
> yes,
> where are you going with yourself,
> with your love?

Oh! My Dear Sweet Love
> where are you going,
> where is your journey taking you,
> where are you going with you,
> yes,
> where is your anguish taking you?

Oh! Cry My Love,
> cry with all your heart,
> cry with your heart
> and let all your pain out,
> cry until you make the rivers flow and the oceans over flow,
> cry until you fall down to the deepest depths,
> and cry out for God,
> cry out for God so loud
> that you cannot be ignored!

And God, Love, Faith and Spirit
> will come to you,
> and make you one with God,
> one in love with God,
> in love with your essence which is God,
> one in forgiving essence
> and acceptance of yourself
> and me
> and all beings
> and one in love with God!

And, my Dear Sweet Love,
> this is where you are going
> on your journey
> to the essence of
> Love, Faith, Forgiveness, Compassion, and God!

And so it is! Amen!
w. j. scheck
santa ana
5 nov 1999

YOU ARE

You are
>   wonderful and full of love,
>   you are
>   just love.

You are
>   me too,
>   and
>   we are
>   one in
>   love,
>   one in
>   our love.

You are
>   wonderful,
>   so very wonderful,
>   and
>   your beauty
>   shines pure and true,
>   you are
>   my dream
>   come true.

And I love you!

You are
>   you
>   and
>   wonderful too,
>   you are
>   the essence
>   of dreams
>   of love
>   that
>   becomes true.
And I love you!
w.j. scheck
santa ana
25 oct 99

ALL OF MY LIFE I HAVE KNOWN GOD

All of my life I have known God,
  in many ways,
  God is magnificent and wonderful,
  for God is apart of me
  and always loves me.

In my dream world
  I know the presence of God,
  God is within me and without me,
  and I know that I will always be with God.

·For this is my right,
  for this is my being,
  and this is who I am,
  one with my total being,
  one with God,
  and always I feel the warmth
  of the love of God within me,
  and I will always know
  that there's nothing better
  than the essence of God
  in my heart,
  in my soul
  in all my being
  when I enter dreamland.
  I know God
  as I open up the portal of my existence
  I find God within me
  and without me
  and in all things.

I know that this is
  all true,
  because I am here on earth,
  and in my dreams
  in many dimensions,
  I am in the dimension of love.
  I am in the dimension of heaven,
  I am in the dimension of wonderful,

The Glory

I am the mention of essence,
I am a new dimension of all there is,
this is the purpose of my existence
to realize my dreams
that I am here in the inner and outer world
of all existences
in all dimensions
wherever I go
I always will be.

When you know God,
　　　　you will realize this
　　　　and you will walking on your journey
　　　　to become one with God
　　　　and be in the light
　　　　when
　　　　you realize your journey has been completed
　　　　here on earth
　　　　you will transcend into heaven
　　　　and still be able to walk in all dimensions
　　　　and to talk to God
　　　　and visualize all that there is.

And so it is!

w.j. scheck
santa ana
3 august 2000

BECOME ONE WITH A MIND OF GOD

Become one with the mind of god,
        become one with your mind,
        become one with God,
        and yet know,
        there are many forces
        that do not want you to be divine,
        and with god.

When you walk with god,
        you are one with the Mind of God,
        you will become known to God.

And , some will not like you,
        and others will hate you
        because they are not with god,
        they will destroy you,
        but God will always love you
        and be with you,
        and the pain imposed upon you by evil,
        will soon go,
        and you will be with God.

Do not be afraid,
        for God is always with you,
        and evil can never destroyed you,
        when your mind is with God's mind,
        your essence will exist in Love
        and with God.

w.j. scheck
4 august 2000
santa ana

GOD CREATED YOU

You are beauty,
> you are love,
> and you are all these things,
> because God created you and is a part of you.

You are all
> that there is
> and ever will be
> for you were created by God
> to be just that!

You are
> the sun,
> the moon,
> and
> the stars,
> the waterfalls,
> the ocean,
> and
> the elements of
> fire,
> air,
> water,
> earth,
> and
> the directions of
> east,
> south,
> west,
> north,
> above and below,
> you are all of these things!

And you are love,
> that is everything you are is God's beauty
> and gift of love.

For this is
> what God created
> in God's creation you.

w.j. scheck
4 august 2000
santa ana

FREEDOM IS LOVE

Freedom comes
        to those who think freedom,
        is the right way,
        the right path.

We cannot buy freedom,
        or fight for freedom,
        we can only follow
        the right way,
        the right path.

The path to freedom is love,
        love that makes all us free,
        free forever more.

Love that opens our hearts to others,
        that makes our life full of beauty,
        that last forever now in our hearts.

Yes, freedom is love,
        and love is our essence
        which is our God
        and freedom is Our Mind,
        the Mind of god
        which is one with us,
        and God.

And so it is!

AMEN!

w.j. scheck
3 july 2000
santa ana

INIFINITE EXPANDING LOVE ALL YOUR DAYS

I came to you in your mind,
        which is the light of all knowing,
        which is me,
        you,
        your essence,
        what you call God

I am your inner self,
        your god,
        the temple
        of ever lasting love and light.

I am all these things,
        and I always will be
        I am "The All"
        the infinite living in mind,
        I am what you call God.

I am here for you,
        and always have been
        for I am in you,
        apart of you,
        I am your "All",
        your mind,
        and I bring you love.

Know me,
        and you will know yourself
        as a part of God,
        God essence,
        and you will know
        infinite expanding love all your days.

Amen!

w.j. scheck
santa ana
5 august 2000

THIS ONENESS

I became one with "The All",
        and every part of me,
        my essence came
        from the mind of "The All".

I looked at the world
        through the eyes of the infinite love
        "the mind"
        of "The All",
        and
        all I saw
        was beauty to
        for this is
        all there is.

When I spoke,
        I spoke the words of "The All"
        and
        I spoke words
        of love.

When I touch you,
        I touch you
        with the warm beauty
        of my love,
        my essence,
        and you
        where healed
        through love.

For all this is true,
        for I am you
        and we are all apart
        of "The All",
        and we are all blessed
        with this oneness.
·And so it is.
w.j scheck
santa ana
6 august 2000

EVIL IS ILLUSION THAT DOES NOT HAVE TO BE

Oh! I came from the stars,
    and I knew it was true
    that I have always been.

I came to earth for all of mankind,
    and
    I saw things
    I dare not describe
    for they were in not of God.

I thought how could this be
    for all is of God,
    then I cried
    for I realize
    that I was of God
    and within me too
    was the power
    of good and evil,
    like these earth being.

And I wept for awhile
    because I could not believe
    that all of this beauty
    could also be evil.

This is when I awakened
    as to why I came here
    as a stranger in a strange land
    that is my love ones
    to tell you of the beauty
    that is always here for you,
    always,
    and
    evil is an illusion that does not have to be.

w.j. scheck
santa ana
7 august 2000

REBORN IN LOVE

I am reborn in love,
     I am spirit,
     and my physical body
     means nothing to me.

I am with "The All", "The Infinite Mine".

Although,
     I am standing here
     before you in body,
     take a close look
     and see my spirit
     through your own essence
     and know me as spirit.

I am reborn in love,
     and I am here for you,
     know me
     for I am here
     to be with you
     in love.

See me,
     my spirit in love
     in all things.

Join me in spirit and love,
     and be with me in love,
     with the oneness of love,
     the oneness
     of "The All",
     the "Infinite Living Mind",
     GOD!

And be reborn with me
     and in me,
     and in LOVE!
w.j. scheck
santa ana
8 August 2000

SING WITH ME!

Sing with ME,
        with ME,
        sing in joy,
        sing in love,
        sing the song of songs,
        always be in joy,
        always be with ME in joy,
        sing out to joy and beauty
        that GOD created for us,
        hold your hands up high,
        bring the LIGHT of GOD
        into you
        and never forget
        you are singing with JOY,
        with GOD!

Sing with your heart,
        sing with your heart.
        hold your hands up high
        to the LIGHT
        let it enter you
        penetrate you,
        never forgetting
        that the LIGHT
        is GOD
        and know
        that your songs of joy
        will revel
        throughout the cosmos
        and always know
        that your songs of happiness and joys
        are songs,
        sung to you by GOD
        for you
        to sing
        to the universe,
        and
        to ALL THAT IS AND EVER WILL BE!

And when this happens
        always feel the love of God
        within you
        and always know
        GOD is of you

and there for you
and always
has been,
when you know
this THRUTH,
you will always be embraced
by the love of GOD.

Never give up SINGING the song of songs
and sing to GOD,
and feel God's love penetrating your soul
and always know
that GOD
is there for you
and you are there for GOD
for the real purpose
you are here on earth
is that your are God's manifestation of GOD on earth
for this is what GOD and YOU are all about,
YOU are GOD on earth.

And my LOVE as above, so is below,
YOU are the manifested of GOD on earth,
you are here to partake
in all of the beauty and love,
GOD created for you,
and to sing the songs of songs
and to sing in joy and love
continuously
forever more.

YOU,
my love,
are here to partake
in this wonder
and to expressed joy and happiness
for this is your role
for this was why you were created
and this is GOD'S way
of giving you
LOVE!

w.j. scheck
santa ana
8 august 2000

GOD IS ALWAYS WITH YOU!

Where is God, where is God,
       when you are all alone,
       why, why,
       are you alone,
       don't you know
       that God has always been with you,
       within and without you
       and is always encompass you.

Don't you know this?

God has always encompass you
       and been apart of you,
       God has always been with you.

God has
       always been
       with you,
       and God
       will always be
       with you,.

Don't you know this?

You are not alone,
       and God has always
       been your essence.

You are with God,
       and God is always
       with you.

Don't you know this?

Never fear
       for no harm can ever come to you,
       for you are always with God,
       and God is always with you.

Amen!
w.j. scheck
santa ana
9 august 2000

THERE IN PEACE AND LOVE IS A PLACE

We all have a place,
　　　　a place in our hearts
　　　　where we go to be loved.

A place of comfort and joy,
　　　　a place that makes us feel good,
　　　　and always brings us happiness.

This place is in our hearts and souls,
　　　　it is a place of oneness with ourselves,
　　　　with love and God.

Close your eyes,
　　　　and go into your heart,
　　　　and you will find you,
　　　　God,
　　　　and love.

Now close your eyes,
　　　　and you are there in peace and love
　　　　a very special place with God.

Amen!

w.j. scheck
santa ana
21 february 2000

BEING LOVE

Do you want it to happen,
        do you want your dreams
        to come true?

Then,
        make it happen,
        make it happen with love,
        love that is the maker of dreams.

Make love to yourself and everyone,
        make love happen,
        make your dreams of love,
        make love to everyone.

Yes,
        make love by being love,
        love that comes from the heart,
        from the center, from God.

Yes,
        always make love
        by being love
        and you and your dreams
        will always come true,
        BEING LOVE!

w.j. scheck
santa ana
20 february 2000

WHAT ARE WE?

.We are what we are,
        not much more than that,
        we just our,
        but sometimes we forget our essence,
        and try to be more,
        we try to be more,
        then love,
        we become hate!

And then we forget
        our essence of love,
        and become hate,
        because we forget
        who we are.

Hate is not bad,
        just a continuation of love,
        but it is better to always
        to return to our essence of love,
        as soon as possible,
        for then we are one with God,
        once again with God
        and in our essence of love.

Yes,
        we are what we are,
        and that is love!

That is what we are!

w.j. scheck
santa ana
4 march 2000

LET THE RAIN FALL

Let the rain fall
      and wash away
      your sorrow,
      let the rain fall
      and wash away
      your tears.

My sweet little ones,
      for the rain purifies your souls
      and brings love back
      The to your heart.

Yes,
      let the rain fall down upon you,
      encompass you
      and purify your heart.

And,
      then your essence will begin anew,
      and love will encompass you.

w.j. scheck
santa ana
6 mar 2000

ATUM - THE ONE WHO LOVES YOU

Now, it is your time
       to know who I am,
       I am ATUM,
       the one who created
       all of this for you.

I am the one
       who created you in my mind,
       I am ATUM,
       The Creator of all there is
       and will be.

I am everything,
       I am all beauty,
       wonder,
       and love,
       there is none
       but me.

When you know me,
       you are truly
       reborn
       in my glory
       and love.

For there is nothing
       but me,
       ATUM,
       and
       I am
       LOVE.

And you are
       apart of me,
       my creation
       and I am
       apart of you
       in my love for you.

I have created
　　　　all of this for you,
　　　　fire, air, water, earth,
　　　　all the directions,
　　　　above and below.

I have made the sun,
　　　　all the stars,
　　　　and all the cosmos
　　　　for you to be apart
　　　　of my glory and love
　　　　for you.

Be a part of this
　　　　all your days on earth,
　　　　and be reborn
　　　　in my love and glory for you,
　　　　and never be afraid to leave this earth
　　　　this is for there is much more to come,
　　　　much more love and beauty
　　　　when you are one with me ATUM,
　　　　the creator of the "ALL"
　　　　the one who loves you.

w.j. scheck
santa ana
10 august 2000

YOUR INNER TEMPLE

I command you,
>go into your inner temple,
>go within,
>and find yourself,
>your essence,
>your love
>your GOD!

Live in your temple in peace,
>and make your dreams and desires known
>to GOD
>and they will be manifested!

Open your mind to GOD
>within you
>and you will co-create with GOD
>and make your dreams and desires
>come true!

Manifest
>love,
>beauty
>and peace
>for yourself
>and the cosmos!

Change everything you feel
>into love
>and peace!

Be apart of this of this
>GOD within
>and make all of this true
>for you
>and
>all of mankind!

w.j. scheck
santa ana
11 august 2000

YOU ARE THE SUN

When the SUN shines down upon you,
>and you feel the warmth,
>love,
>and the pure goodness
>you are feeling life
>and creation,
>you are feeling the your purityof love,
>and the beauty of "The All"!

And when this happens,
>give thanks,
>and praise
>for
>THE ALL,
>ATUM,
>GOD
>has created this
>for you.

When you experienced
>this "Great Mystery",
>you experience the love of God,
>and then you walk your journey on earth
>in love,
>in peace,
>and
>in loving kindness.

Give love to all things,
>be like God,
>be God,
>let pure warm love
>radiate from you
>as if you were the SUN,
>GOD
>for you are!

And so it is!

w.j.scheck

santa ana

13 august 2000

BUT ONE PLACE!

There is but one place,
> and it is the "Infinite Loving Mind,
> and it is yours
> to be reborn
> in love.

You are this "Mind",
> you are it
> and it
> is
> what is
> known
> to you
> as
> God,
> Atum

There is but one place,
> and it is the "Infinite Loving Mind"
> it is yours,
> for it is found within you
> and exist in your essence
> for all of time.

There is but one place,
> and it is the "Infinite Loving Mind of God",
> and it is yours to be reborn in love!

And love is where you want to be,
> love is the place you want to be in,
> in your mind,
> and you want to be reborn in love
> and loving kindness
> for
> that
> is your right!

You have
> THE RIGHT
> to be reborn
> in loving kindness!

And so it is
w.j.scheck
santa ana
14 august 2000

AND I WILL ALWAYS LOVE YOU!

When they will ever know,
       when will they never know me,
       I hope soon.

For I have always been here
       for you to know.

Yes,
       I have always been here
       for you to know.

Yes,
       I have always been with you,
       all your essence,
       and when you open your heart
       you will know me

For I am your love,
       your loving kindness,
       your essence of love,
       your God within
       and without you!

I am you and all things,
       and you are apart of me!

And I will
       always
       love
       you!

w.j. scheck
santa ana
15 august 2000

IN THE ESSENCE OF GOD

How do you
　　　　get to know
　　　　the Mind of God?

By knowing yourself,
　　　　for your Mind
　　　　is
　　　　the Mind of God!

.How do you become reborn?

By living in the essence
　　　　of the Mind of God
　　　　which is within you,
　　　　without you
　　　　and all around you!

You are reborn
　　　　when your Mind recognizes,
　　　　it is one
　　　　with the Mind of God,
　　　　and always has been!

And when you are reborn
　　　　in the essence of God,
　　　　you become all there is
　　　　to be and ever will be!

w.j. scheck
santa ana
16 august 2000

GO INTO YOURSELF

Go into yourself
       and find out who you are,
       say hello,
       and thank you to you
       and God.

Get to know who you are,
       and say I love you
       to all things and beings.

Live in love
       and acceptance of God's love
       for you and all things,
       and always welcome love
       into your heart.

Let love in
       and be part of you.

Now
       that you are love,
       you are a co-creator with God,
       and this is as it should be,

You and us
       and God are one in love.

And so it is!

w.j. scheck
santa ana
6 september 2000

˙A VERY SPECIAL DAY

Today is your birthday,
           a very special day
           when you came into your
           own
           on earth,
           and a day of remembrance.

For you were born out of God's love for you
           to experience the beauty of earth
           and the knowledge of haven.

You were born in God's love
           and God's love
           is always with you.

You are a beautiful creation of love!

And today on this very special day
           God has given you to me
           to love
           and hold
           closely
           to my heart!

A day
           when I can say
           I love you with all my heart
           and I always will .

A day
           when I can give thanks to God
           for creating you.

A day
           when I can give thanks to you
           for all the love you have given me!
w.j. scheck
santa ana
7 september 2000

THE LIGHT IS SHINY

The light is shiny and it is you,
  but you do not know that,
  so you ignore the light
  and walk around in desperation.

Then all of sudden something happens to you,
  and you begin to feel the light inside you,
  and it truly is a miracle
  for you have never felt anything like this before,
  you are amazed at the beauty you find within you,
  you are truly amazed at the beauty of God inside you.

And you ask,
  how could this be
  that there is so much beauty and love inside me,
  how could this be
  that God created this wonderful miracle
  for me
  inside me
  and for me to enjoy
  and have with me
  for all of eternity.

Oh! Thank you God
  for this miracle of love and beauty.

Oh! Thank you God for my existence
  to feel this beauty, love, and unity
  and thank you for all that there is.

Amen.

w.j. scheck
santa ana
12 september 2000

IN THE NOW!

There is but one place,
> and it is here,
> now in this moment
> and in you.

Yes,
> it is,
> it is that moment of now,
> with no past or future,
> it is you in the now of nothing,
> in his the moment with God!

Yes,
> you are there,
> you are always there
> in the now
> in the moment
> with God!

So much of the moment
> is beauty and love,
> so much love
> that
> you are overwhelmed with it,
> and you truly know God!

Yes,
> you are there,
> your always there
> in the now
> in the moment
> with God!

And so it.

w.j. scheck
santa ana
8 sep 2000

I AM THAT I AM

I am in the now
        because I am I,
        the inner consciousness
        that observes and creates me.

I am that I am,
        I am me and all there is
        for I am that I am,
        I am the word,
        the creator of all.

I observe and change me,
        my reality at will
        for I am the creator of it all.
I marvel
        at what I have created
        and will create,
        and I am all there is.

And so it is!

Amen!

w.j. scheck
santa ana
13 september 20000

SO MUCH LOVE

There are so many,
       many wonders,
       and so much love,
       that we should
       take the time
       to give thanks,
       thanks to God
       all of this!

There is so much love
       for you and I
       and for all of us
       that we should always
       live in love,
       love that always is!

When we walk
       on our journey on earth,
       we should see love in all things,
       in God's presence everywhere!

For we all are God's love
       and of God!

Because this is what we co-created for ourselves
       with God,
       for we all are of the mind,
       the loving mind of God!

And so it is!

w.j. scheck
santa ana
7 september 2000

ONE LIGHT

There is but one light,
        and it is the light
        which is God
        and gives life to our souls!

It is the light of the word of creation,
        the energy vibration
        that makes us
        and the cosmos and all there is.

We are the creation
        of the mind of God,
        that
        just is!

And we try to explain it
        but we cannot
        because it
        just is!

It simply is a knowing
        that all this is true,
        and always was
        and is!

w.j.scheck
santa ana
14 september 2000

THE PLACE CALLED "I"

There is no place,
　　　　but the place " the" I,
　　　　I is the place
　　　　of the mind of God,
　　　　within you
　　　　and without you.

"I" a is the mind of God
　　　　which is
　　　　your loving God source.

Your place is
　　　　and always been
　　　　in the Mind of God,
　　　　for you truly are
　　　　a creation of God's Mind.

Live in God's Mind,
　　　　and be apart of God's love.

This is your place
　　　　under the Sun,
　　　　and it always has been.

Look to the source
　　　　in you
　　　　and star
　　　　into the
　　　　Sun
　　　　and see God's love
　　　　radiate to you
　　　　and see the rays penetrate you
　　　　in love
　　　　and in the "I"
　　　　of God!

w.j. scheck
santa ana
15 september 2000

FIRE MOUNTAIN

Essence went up to the mountain - FIRE MOUNTAIN.
      A place where the mountain meets the sky,
      where the clouds are in haven,
      a place were Essence speaks to God.
      This mountain is in a place not far from here,
      not far from our souls.
      This place is a mountain of beauty,
      but also a mountain of fire.
      A place were the fire meets the soul,
      a place where God meets man.
      It is not easy to get to this mountain,
      sometimes one must walk trail of tears
      to reach the top of the mountain.
      Essence walk this trail of tears,
      essence walked many millenniums
      up this mountain to find God.

At first Essence made many trips to the mountain,
      and he would just looked at the magnificent mountain
      and stare into the heavens above
      for Essence did not know
      if God would permit him
      to travel up the mountain.
      The mountain appears to be crystal white
      and yet it has all the colors of the universe
      when the sun shines on it,
      and at night
      it is a white as the moon
      with hues of dark blue.
      The mountains calls to Essence
      in an enchaining manners
      and asks Essence
      to travel on the trails
      to become a part of the mountain.

Essence first walk on the mountain many thousands of years ago
      when Essence appeared on earth
      send by God to be a part of the Earth.
      He knew that someday

he would have to make the pilgrimage
up the mountain
to become one
with God again.

The journey began many thousands of years ago
when Essence learned the ways of the Earth.
His earth brothers taught him
about pain and suffering,
about greed and hate,
about war and destruction.
In his heart Essence cry tears after tears
because this horror was all knew to him
because he knew
that God did not want him
or mankind to behave
in this manner.
The tears filled the
streams,
rivers,
lakes
and oceans
with water
and
Essence heart was sick
because he learned
the ways of the Earth.

The earth to him was a very strange,
beautiful,
but a savage place.
A place where he was a stranger,
he was a stranger in a strange land,
sent by God to make his earth walk.
At times Essence thought
God had forsaken him
because God send him
to this strange place called
Earth.
But,
he knew that
if he could walk up

Fire Mountain,
walk the paths
that he would find God
and God would bless him,
for Essence was send on a journey by God,
a journey to learn the ways of the Earth
and to change the earth,
to raise the consciousness of the earth
with loving kindness
and to show everyone the path
up Fire Mountain to God.

Beginning his journey on Fire Mountain,
Essence came to the amber path
of much beauty and hope.
He step onto this path
and he felt his heart pounding with joy
for he had felt these vibrations before.
He closed his eyes and saw a reflection
of his past life
with the Essence of God.
He recalled the love of God
and his love for all of God's creations
especially his cosmic family
whom he left behind in order
to make his Earth Walk.
He especially missed their love,
kindness and the warmth of their souls.
Tears fell from his eyes because
he missed his cosmic family a great deal.
But,
he knew
that once he completed his Earth Walk
he could be with his family again.

However, he began to cry in anguish because he realized
that during his absence the forces of
Universal Evil
destroyed
his family
because he was not there to protect them
for Essence is a powerful

Cosmic Warrior,
but God sent him on his earth journey,
and he was not there to save his family
from the most horrible of faiths.
He cried many tears
because now he could feel
in the amber vibrations the horrible anguish
his cosmic family felt
as they died at the hands of the forces of
Evil.
He materialized himself
into a flash of white light
and travel to his family cosmic home
only to find that they were no more.
All he could feel was the Energy of Evil,
and he cried
for now he learned the meaning
of pain and suffering and hate,
for now he learned
the ways of the Earth.
He learned to hate and seek revenge.

But, God called him back to Earth
and back to the
amber path on Fire Mountain.
Essence cried a thousand tears,
until no more tears would come,
and then he sat looking into the sun,
burning the sun onto his retinas,
burning the light of God
into his soul.
He sat on the amber path
in deep contemplation
with the light of God
entering his soul.
As the light of God enter his soul,
the light turn to emerald green
and his heart became warm
with love and passion.

He open is eyes and saw an emerald green path,
a path that lead him through a forest on the mountain,

a beautiful forest full of love.
He saw a lovely image of his love,
his wife whom he thought had perished,
but, she had not.
He went up to her,
kissed her on the forehead, and said,
"I love you, my dear sweet love. I love you very much".
She put her arms around him, and said,
"I love you too my dear sweet love".
She said,
"walk with me along the emerald path of creation,
walk with me to along the path of love to our place on the
mountain".
She lead Essence to a waterfall,
a beautiful waterfall,
where the sun created a magnificent rainbow
of the pure colors of love.
The waterfall drop
into a beautiful aquamarine lake
of crystal clear water.
In the lake he saw his children swimming,
playing, and laughing like children do.
They saw him and left the water
running to his arms crying
"Daddy, we love you, we missed you,
where have you been,
why did you leave us.
Please never leave us again."
He put his arms run his little girl and boy and said,
"I love you too and I will never leave you again".
His heart and soul where full of joy,
the joy of love and happiness.
His love for his wife and children
was immeasurable
and he thank God
for this wonderful moment in time.
He was overwhelm with joy and happiness
for he was with his family again.

His mind was confused for now he did not know
if he was living a dream,
if all of life was a dream.

He did not know
what was his true reality!
Did his family parish or where they alive?
Was he alive?
Who was he?
Where was he?

He did not know where he was
for he was in
a cosmic dream of life,
a dream of no beginnings and no ends,
a dream that would take him
up Fire Mountain to God.
He was stunned for he thought he was truly out of his mind,
but he did not know where his mind was.
He was floating in a cosmic dream,
floating in the universe with the stars,
floating in the space of all times,
he was in timeless space.
He was floating into his essence,
floating to God,
and he was stunned
for he was in nothingness nothing.
He entered the nothingness of God,
and cried out
" Oh, God
what am I,
where am I,
who am I?"
There was no answer,
just the VOID
and he was truly stunned
with no reaction,
just floating in the VOID.
Then, he heard a voice saying
"come back come back to Fire Mountain
where you belong,
where the mountain meets the heaven,
where you will find your essence,
where you will find your God.
He cried out,
"but how, how can I get back to the mountain,

how can I
get out of the VOID".
Then, he heard the answer from a the voice of GOD,
"open your eyes,
open your essence
and you will find yourself
back on Fire Mountain.
He open his eyes
and he was on the mountain
and ONE WITH GOD,
ONE WITH THE VOID!

w. j. scheck
santa ana
13 july1998,
12 August 1998
& 28 september 2000

TO KNOW WILL YOU ARE

There is no time
>   like the present time
>   to know you who you are
>   for now is
>   the only existence
>   there is!

Live as long as you can
>   perhaps
>   forever
>   in the now,
>   and experience it
>   with all you can.

Yes,
>   always live in
>   and be apart of it,
>   and know
>   who you are!

For you are nothing
>   and so am I,
>   nothing
>   but
>   a creation
>   in
>   the Mind of the All,
>   God!

And
>   as long
>   as we remember that
>   and live that,
>   we know
>   who we are,
>   and we are one with God!

And this is true!

And always will be!
w.j. scheck
santa ana
18 september 2000

THE DAY I BECAME I

Today I became I,
      and not me,
      and used my I
      to will my me,
      and took charge
      of me.

For me,
      is not me,
      but all those influences
      that entering me,
      and made me think
      that I was me.

How strange
      to finally realized
      who I am
      I am will
      and all those things
      that are all will,
      and manifesting
      my will tells me
      what to do
      and what to manifest!

How wonderful!

And thank you God!

w.j. schedck
santa ana
19 september2000

LOOK AT ME

Look at me,
        look at me,
        and say hello
        to me
        with
        all
        your
        heart.

Say hello
        with
        all
        your
        love
        for I need
        your love
        so very much
        like
        you
        need
        mine.

I am
        here
        for you,
        and
        I have
        always been,
        I am here
        with
        all
        my
        love.

See me
        all around you,
        see the son and the moon,
        and feel the air, water, and earth,
        I exist

for you
and
I
have always
love you.

Love me
TOO
by being apart of me
and living in love
in all
that I have created
for you!

w.j. scheck
santa ana
20 september 2000

FAITH IS TRUTH!

As you believe,
      you are,
    believe in it whatever it is,
      and it will be true,
      a miracle.

Believe
      and make it a habit,
      make it faith,
      and you will control it all.

With faith
      you will control the cosmos
      and be a co-creator with me,
      and you will know me
      who is you, God!

Faith is truth,
      and truth is me,
      God!

Miracles
      are the result
      of the truth
      which is faith
      in God,
      and you will be
      a co-creator
      with
      God!

w.j scheck
santa ana
21 september 2000.

ALL THINGS

I have a thought,
        a mind,
        that creates all things,
        which can be of beauty and love.

Love that is so pure and true,
        surely it must come from God,
        the God that is the ALL.

All that I am is of God,
        God's mind
        and my mind
        is the creation
        of God's mind.

How wonderful this is
        to live and exist
        in the Mind of God
        Love!

All this beauty and love
        is for me in you,
        all of us!

All this is God's mind creating it!

How wonderful!

Thank you God,
        thank you
        for all of this!

w.j. scheck
santa ana
25 september 2000

A GOOD THING

No matter what you think,
      your thoughts are
      of the mind of God
      who knows all.

Some may be puzzled by this
      because their thoughts are evil,
      but God knows all
      and gives you free will!

Evil is there in your mind
      But you can choose love,
      And
      POLARIZE
      your thoughts
      in loving kindness!

This is God's gift
      of the mind to you,
      to have,
      to know
      the OPPOSITE
      and
      to live
      in love.

And this is a good thing
      and
      THANKS
      should be given
      to GOD
      for this!

Amen!

w.j. scheck
santa ana
26 september 2000

SO EASY

When we wonder,
>   we know,
>   we know,
>   we are
>   a creation
>   of the Mind
>   of the All-God!

We know
>   that
>   everything
>   is
>   of the Mind
>   of God!

>   Yet we

>   don't believe

>   it,

>   we make

>   our spirit journey

>   more difficult

>   for

>   we do not want

>   to believe

>   it,

>   we are of

>   God!

>   How strange

>   that

>   we want

to make

everything

so difficult

when all we have

to be

is of God

of God's MIND

and

CREATION!

It is so easy

    and full

    of love

    and

    abundance

    when we remember

    THIS!

Yes,

    so easy
    and so much love
    and abundance
    when we are of
    THIS!

Amen!

w.j. scheck
santa ana
27 september 2000

WONDER OF LOVE

There is so much to think about
        and to wonder about
        and the most wonderful thing
        of all
        is that
        God is here
        for us to have.

Yes, everything is here
        for us because
        God made it
        that way!

All of it
        is ours,
        of all it
        and
        we are here
        to live in love and kindness,
        and to enjoy all of this!

Yes,
        we are here to live
        in this wonder of love
        that is our SPIRIT
        and our God!

w.j. scheck
28 september 2000

THE ETERNAL YOU

I am the eternal you,
> your inner temple
> of your essence,
> I am what you know as
> UNITY,
> love,
> and
> kindness!

I am always
> with you
> in all your thoughts
> in all your being
> for I am you!

You don't know this sometimes
> and you wonder
> who you are,
> and
> then
> you know.

You know you are me,
> And I am you
> and we are
> I AM THAT I AM,
> the words of God,
> the thoughts of God,
> the love and beauty
> of God's mind!

And so it is.

Amen!

w.j. scheck
santa ana
29 september 2000

POWER OF LOVE
Life

        is but an opportunity
        to live and feel the power
        of love within you,
        to know others and God in love.

Take advantage
        of this opportunity
        and be
        in love.

Love

        That
        KNOWS
        no boundaries
        and
        is
        kindness
        to all!

Take a moment
        to be in love
        with
        everything,
        everyone,
        and
        GOD!

Feel

        this feeling
        in you,
        and make it
        your
        HOLLIES OF HOLIES!

And give thanks and praise
        to GOD
        for giving you
        the opportunity
        to be a part of this!
Amen!
w.j. scheck
santa ana
3 october 2000

FOR EVER I AM GOD

·Now,

        I know
        there is
        no place,
        no place
        at all,
        but me,
        my existence
        is me
        for whatever
        that means.

Yes,

        I exist,
        and
        I am,
        me,
        but
        where am I
        but
        in
        the Mind
        of God.

Yes,

        both my "I" and "me",
        exist in God's mind,
        what a shocked
        to find out
        my very existence
        is in God's mind,
        and "I" and "me"
        are
        of
        God!

Yes,

       a creation of God
       solely existing
       in God,
       and my nothingness,

I am

       also
       God!

How strange it is

       to know this truth,
       and to keep it
       with me
       for all time,
       that
       I am
       of
       God!

w.j. scheck
santa ana
4 october 2000

OVER THERE

Over there,
       over there,
       there is a place for us,
       a place called love,
       and
       it is
       in our hearts
       in our souls,
       our spirits,
       our God.

It is waiting for us
       to enter
       and
       to be apart of us,
       for now
       and
       for ever!

Oh, please take a journey to it,
       to love,
       and let it open
       your essence
       to all of us,
       and
       most important
       to God.

Feel LOVING-KINDNESS
       in yourself
       and give thanks
       to ATUM
       The ALL
       for this
       is your purpose
       to live
       in love forever more
       in the essence of
       GOD,
       our lover!
w.j. scheck
santa ana
5 Oct 2000

A DREAM FLOWING FROM YOU

Life is
>
> but a dream
> flowing from you,
> free flowing
> from your essence,
> and smiling
> down upon you
> in wonder and grace
> giving you love.

A dream
>
> that knows
> no bounds,
> or illusions
> for it is
> your real you,
> your real essence
> of whom
> you are
> and always
> will be.

Hold onto
>
> your dreams
> for this is
> God speaking
> to you
> a message
> from God of
> love,
> wonder,
> and grace.

This is your time
>
> for your mortal body
> to feel and experience
> all there is
> of this beauty and love
> God created

for you,
and for
your immortal soul
to carry with you
for all of time,
until once again
you are
one with god,
totally one
with God's essence!

What a

wonderful and joyful journey,
enjoy it.
to its fullest,
and give
praise and thanks
to God
for
all of it!

Amen!

w.j. scheck
santa ana
6 october 2000

TURN AWAY

We are here
      and god created it
      all for us,
      the Good Earth to nurture us
      the heavens to give us life and direction.

We are here
      to be apart of this miracle of God's love,
      but some forget this,
      and take no part in it,
      they destroy the love
      God has given them.

And then cry out
      in anguish
      why has God
      forsaken them,
      when God has not,
      they have forsaken
      God's love.

These are
      strange and sad beings
      who populate this haven on earth,
      and made it a hell
      for themselves and others,
      what EVIL they are,
      but God will forgive them,
      and give them love
      and haven again
      on earth
      when they turned
      away from EVIL,
      and open
      their hearts
      to God.
Amen!
w.j. scheck
santa ana
9 october 2000

A TIME OF MAGIC

There once was a time
> when all we did was love,
> love everything and everyone.

A time
> of magic
> when we were in love,
> when the sun was bright,
> and the water pure
> and the stars shiny and bright.

A time
> when I was a child
> and would look
> at the cosmos
> and see love and beauty
> all around me.

A time
> of sweet innocence
> when all there was,
> was me
> and God
> and Love!

A time
> of such great beauty and love
> that I was overwhelmed with it,
> and
> I know
> that
> soon I will return
> to that moment
> of pure beauty and love
> and my God!

How wonderful
> it will be
> to be in this magic time again!

w.j. scheck
santa ana
10 October 2000

OPEN YOUR MIND

Open your mind
> to God,
> do this and feel God,
> it is a joyous thing,
> and full of wonder.

Just give up
> your pretenses
> and
> be one
> with God.

Forget
> who you are,
> forget
> your ego
> and
> all
> of
> your
> worldly
> possessions,
> and
> be
> in the sweet moment
> of your creation
> with
> God!

Know this joy,
> live
> in
> the
> now,
> and
> always
> be
> of
> God!

Yes,

      my love one
      open your mind,
      and souls,
      and hearts to me
      your God
      that
      created
      you
      and
      be
      apart of me
      all your days
      and all your essence
      for this is your gift
      of my Love for you!

w.j. scheck
santa ana
12 October 2000

THE BEAUTY OF BEING

I know now
> the beauty of being
> of being mortal,
> yet immortal,
> I know
> I will exist
> forever more,
> yet I have
> never
> existed!

I have a body,
> which
> I can touch
> and see,
> and a Mind of Energy,
> which is of God,
> the Mind of God.

I look
> at all
> that is around me
> and
> I marvel
> at the good and evil!

How interesting
> it all is
> for it is
> my illusion,
> my creation,
> and
> none
> of
> it
> matters
> for
> it
> is not real
> only

an
illusion
of
my
thoughts!

As time passes,
I know
I must give up
my body
and
all the
illusions
of
good
and
evil,
and
passe on,
and only be of Mind,
the Mind of God,
how wonderful
and exciting
that will be!

w.j. scheck
santa ana
13 october 2000

WE ARE HERE

We are here,
> but also there,
> we are earth bound,
> yet a part of the above,
> the cosmos!

We are love,
> love from above,
> which comes to us below,
> we are all a part of it,
> all of it,
> but sometimes
> we do not realize
> it
> until we look
> at the heavens above
> and then we know.

Then,
> we know,
> we are always with god,
> and god
> is always with
> us!

It
> is a miracle,
> all this wonder!

And it is
> for us to have
> all of our days.

Forever more!

w.j. scheck
santa ana
16 October 2000

WINDOWS OF THE WORLD

When the windows
      of the world
      look down
      upon you
      and you
      are seen.

Who are you?
      What does it mean?
      You may answer
      that you
      do not know
      who we are,
      and then
      you wonder
      who you are!

And what doesn't mean?
      When you
      are seen
      and you
      do not know
      your
      essence!

What does it mean?
      When you are
      but you
      yet you
      do not know
      who you are!

Then,
      the realization
      comes to you,
      and you know,
      you know
      you are
      of God,

     and that is
     who you are!

You are of god,
     and that is
     who you are,
     a miracle!

w.j. scheck
santa ana
17 october 2000

MAGIC TEMPLE

Close your eyes,
        closed them
        and take your journey
        into your magic temple.

Walk inside
        and see into your mind,
        see a circle,
        and within the circle
        a pool of magical blue water.

Look into the water
        and see with your mind
        the past, present, and future,
        see it all.
        for it all
        exist at the same time,
        see whatever you would like,
        see the cosmos,
        all of it.

And be sure to see
        God's love in the magical pool,
        and be amazed
        at the beauty
        of the pure white light of God's love
        coming to you.

And then enter the light
        and be a part of it,
        and know
        this is your inheritance,
        then leave the light
        and depart from the temple,
        open your eyes
        and marvel at it all!

And so it is!

Amen!
w.j. scheck
santa ana
18 october 2000

BETTER THAN LIFE ITSELF

Better than life itself
        is the view
        from your heart,
        the view of what is!

Better than all there is,
        is the view
        from your heart
        which is of love,
        love that is you,
        of God!

When you live
        in this love,
        there is nothing better,
        and it is more
        than earthly life!

It is your
        God essence
        deep
        inside
        of you
        taking you
        away from
        the illusions
        of life,
        and
        giving you
        beauty
        and
        pure love,
        and making
        you one
        with love and
        in love.

How wonderful
>   to be in love,
>   and to see
>   the cosmos
>   with the total love,
>   your eternal love
>   of
>   and
>   from
>   GOD!

Yes,
>   this is better
>   than life itself!

w.j. scheck
santa ana
9 october 2000

GO INTO IT

Go into it,
        your mind,
        your essence,
        and
        what do you see,
        what do you feel?

Think for a minute,
        hold your thoughts,
        your mind
        becomes
        full of nothingness,
        then you become tired
        and almost fall asleep
        but don't sleep,
        fight it off,
        fight hard
        for now
        you are going
        into your
        true you,
        your essence!

And essence
        is what
        you feel,
        you see,
        and
        you are surprised
        for you feel the void
        of nothingness,
        and
        you
        are calm,
        and you feel calm,
        you a feel love,
        a warm love,
        God's love!

And you marvel
>> at this bliss
>> and
>> you
>> become
>> a believer,
>> you
>> are
>> born again
>> in the void,
>> the nothingness of God,
>> God's love,
>> and
>> then
>> you give thanks
>> for this miracle
>> and
>> become
>> one
>> with it
>> with God.

w.j. scheck
santa ana
20 october 2000

NO PRETENSES

Now, there is a moment in time,
      when we are what we are and no more than that,
      we have no pretenses, and we are what we are!

I am you, and you are me,
      and we are of love, of God,
      nothing more or less,
      and this is what we are.

We are an energy that always was,
      and always will be in a moment of time,
      and we are a creation of the Mind of God,
      waiting to happen in a simple short moment,
      and then returning to God's Mind.

And that is what we are and no more.

And so it is as it should and must be.

Amen!

w.j. scheck
santa ana to
23 october 2000

SUMMER

When the wind blows,
     it is
     the summer,
     the summer
     of your
     heart and soul.

You
     at first
     hear the sound
     of the warm wind,
     then you feel it
     encompass you
     and you feel good,
     really good.

And this warmth
     makes you
     feel so good,
     so good inside
     as though
     the warmth of love
     has always been
     with you.

Yes,
     summer
     is here,
     and you feel
     so good,
     yes,
     the summer
     of your heart
     and soul
     is with you
     and you
     are alive
     with warm love,
     which is always

with you.

Yes,

summer
is here,
and
you are alive
with love,
warm love
that comes
to you,
with
the summer wind,
and this is a good thing!

w.j.scheck
santa ana
24 Oct 2000

CARING FOR YOU IN MY MIND

Hello, out there,
> how are you doing,
> I hope OK,
> good,
> for you where meant
> to do
> good!

You know
> I have been caring
> for you in my mind,
> and I know if you accept my love,
> you will be in your essence with me,
> and you will live in bliss with me.

Take your time for there is no rush,
> you have until the end of time to be with me
> for in reality there is no time.

You know
> I care about you
> and will always watch over you
> and you are apart of me
> and I am apart of you!

When you are one
> in your bliss with me,
> you will laugh
> at your pass fears,
> and living in the joy
> of
> my love,
> My Mind!

And so it is.

Amen.
w.j. scheck
santa ana
25 october 2000

YES, JUST DO IT

When we know who and what we are,
        we know we are
        True and Pure Mind,
        the Mind of The All,
        yet we exist somehow
        in a universe of physical things,
        and in many illusions!

And yet,
        we are always
        SEEKING
        to return to our
        True and Pure Mind,
        YES,
        our
        True
        and
        Pure Mind.

We walk many PATHS
        and feel much,
        we are born
        into a body,
        and die
        and pass
        from it,
        then
        we
        are
        Pure
        and
        True
        Mind.

We struggle
        and make
        much
        of our physical existence,
        and then we are no more

in body!
Some see the light
　　　　when in body
　　　　and
　　　　become
　　　　IMMEDIATELY
　　　　One with their Pure and True Mind
　　　　and One with the Mind of The All,
　　　　GOD!

And this is
　　　　an easy thing to do,
　　　　because all we have to do
　　　　is
　　　　do it now,
　　　　YES, JUST DO IT!

w.j. scheck
santa ana
26 october 2000

IMAGINE

I imagine
> what we are,
> when we are
> in a special place,
> and the light shines
> on
> and
> in
> us!

What is this place,
> only you know,
> it may be anywhere
> in
> your heart,
> your soul,
> your mind,
> but
> no matter
> where it is,
> you will
> find
> it!

For it is your
> God place
> where
> you are
> one with god,
> and
> you will always be
> one with God!

There it is,
> so easy,
> now
> do it,
> and
> do it
> with
> love!
Amen
w.j. scheck
santa ana
27 october 2000

RAINING

It is raining now
>and
>how good
>it is
>to hear
>the sound.

It sounds
>so wonderful
>as the water
>falls,
>it is such
>a miracle!

The rain
>has come,
>with
>precious
>water
>for renewal
>and birth!

Soon
>the wild fields
>will be
>emerald green
>and
>the landscape
>will be
>an emerald miracle!

How wonderful
>it is
>and
>thank you
>GOD!

Amen
w.j. scheck
santa ana
27 october 2000

A DAY OF WONDER

Today is a day of wonder,
like many days,
it is
just a day,
just a moment
in time
for me.

But,
I will always
love this day
because
it is
a day,
a moment
that
God
made
for
me!

Yes,
I will breath
in the sweet air
of
life
and
thank
God
for today,
and
for
all
the
moments.

And,

>   I will live this day
>   in beauty and love,
>   and always be in
>   harmony
>   with God's sweet love!

And so it is!

Amen!

w.j. scheck
santa ana
10 february 2000

THE MUNDANE

I think,
>I know,
>I do,
>for
>I have thoughts,
>which are mind,
>and of course someone else,
>GOD's!

How strange it is
>that in my head,
>GOD
>has mundane thoughts,
>like pay the bills,
>and put oil in my car,
>how very strange it is!

But,
>God is taking care of me in the earth world,
>helping me to do and enjoy the things
>that I must do in order to travel
>the path back to God.

Of course,
>I have never left the path or lost it,
>but,
>I just have had many mundane things
>to do!

So,
>when I do the mundane,
>and I practice the mundane
>with the awareness
>GOD
>in my thoughts,
>I am one with
>GOD
>in all things,
>and truly on my
>GOD
>PATH,
>the path of love
>and many, many, small miracles
>every moment of my essence.

w.j. scheck
santa ana
30 october 2000

ENJOY YOUR SORROWS

Think about it now,
        where is your soul going,
        now
        when it is
        ENTRAPPED
        by your body!

But there is more,
        a journey
        of glory and a miracle
        for you and your
        SOUL,
        which is you
        and your essence,
        YES
        a beautiful journey!

And soon
        you will be
        there
        as you travel
        from one dimension to another,
        you will become
        ONE with
        THE ALL!

Don't rush,
        take your time,
        ENJOY,
        ENJOY
        every moment of
        IT,
        most of all enjoyed your
        SORROWS
        for they are giving birth to your
        BLISS,
        Thank
        GOD
        for all of this,

your miracle journey to becoming
ONE
with CREATION,
the Mind of GOD!

How joyous
and wonderful this is,
give thanks and be humble
in your bliss and in your
RETURN!

w.j. scheck
santa ana
31 october 2000

TO BE ONE ONTO GOD

To be one onto GOD,
> you must be like God
> that is in all places
> at all times
> you must
> be mortal
> yet immortal!

You must be
> able to travel
> to all dimensions
> and be in all dimensions!

You must be
> in
> the Holy of Holies!

And you wonder
> how can this be done,
> how can it be?

Simple,
> you are already there,
> you have never not been there
> for you are a creation of God's mind,
> and you have always been in God.

Open
> your mind,
> and you will know
> that this is a wonderful
> pure truth
> of who you are.

w.j. scheck
santa ana
1 November 2000

WE BOTH LAUGHED

It really
    does not
    matter
    anymore,
    you know,
    all that is,
    just is,
    and there
    is no more
    than that!

Yes we try
    and we dream
    but what we want
    is really here now!

You know,
    I once wanted much,
    and then I got it all
    and then what?

I don't know
    and I said,
    you know it does not matter,
    and I said I failed at all,
    and how a wonderful that was,
    and I was tired,
    and God said
    what do we do next,
    and I said what do you mean,
    your are the ONE
    who is supposed to be in charge?

And God laughed,
    a wonderful laugh,
    and said "no",
    "you have free will",
    and I laughed,
    and we both laughed

in wonder and joy
to the end of time!

How amazing
and what a wonderful
miracle
this
all
is!

w.j. scheck
santa ana
2 november 2000

GOD'S WIND

The wind
   is
   blowing
   hard
   now,
   and the leaves
   are falling
   to the
   ground.

It is
   a wonderful
   warm wind
   blowing off
   the desert,
   and blowing
   warmth
   to me.

How nice it is
   the wind,
   so warm
   and tender,
   you can hear
   it
   now
   as it blows
   harder
   and
   harder
   and
   you wonder
   how hard
   it
   can
   below.

Then

       you wonder
       and think,
       just
       about hard blowing wind,
       and think
       what is it all about,
       and then you
       hear a whisper in the wind,
       and you know it is about life,
       and you hear God saying "hello",
       to you,
       and
       then
       you just are
       apart of the hard warm blowing wind,
       and you have no more
       thoughts,
       because
       you
       are just
       in the
       essence
       of
       God's Wind!

w.j. scheck
santa ana
3 november 2000

TO FEEL THIS LOVE

So here we are again,
>> you and I again,
>> and in our moment
>> we are love again,
>> once more
>> in sweet love again.

How wonderful!
>> It is to have this essence again,
>> and to feel this love.

How joyous!
>> It is to be in this sweet essence
>> and to enjoy this bliss.

Oh!
>> How marvelous it is,
>> to be a part of it once again.

To know this
>> sweet tenderness,
>> and feel this love
>> blowing across
>> our essence
>> and being
>> of me,
>> you,
>> us
>> again!

Yes,
>> it is so
>> wonderful and good
>> that I know this essence of love
>> will be with you, me, and us
>> forever,
>> yes,
>> forever,
>> and always again
>> in our hearts!

w.j. scheck
santa ana
6 november 2000

GO INTO THE DIVINE

Go forth now,
> go in to the divine
> and do it.

How wonderful,
> you are apart
> of it now,
> it was easy,
> all you had to do
> was do it.

Yes,
> now you are
> beauty,
> essence,
> love
> and
> all
> these
> things.

Such
> an exciting
> miracle
> you
> are!

Oh!
> How wonderful and exciting
> that
> now
> you
> can
> see
> throughout
> the
> cosmos

You can

> see and feel it all,
> what an exciting miracle,
> and how wonderful it is!

OH!

> Now you are so, so divine
> that God even marvels at it
> and
> truly
> it is
> a wonderful and
> exciting miracle
> that you are!.

w.j. scheck
santa ana
8 november 2000

NOT HERE!

If I were not here,
> where would I be,
> and what would I do
> for I know nothing but here,
> NOW!

How wonderful
> to be
> nothing,
> yet in the here and now,
> how calm it is
> to be of nothing,
> and nothingness!

When I think about it,
> when
> I
> think about having nothing,
> and just being here,
> I
> realize what a miracle,
> and
> I
> am overwhelmed with it!

And that is a good thing
> and an honest thing,
> because now
> I
> am
> nobody,
> and no one cares
> what
> I
> am!

I am in peace and calm,
> and there forever with
> "The All"

in the presence of the Holy of Holies,
in between haven and earth
and yet in my body on earth

Thank you God
    for this
    most wonderful
    of miracles!

Amen

w.j. scheck
santa ana
9 november 2000

·HELLO! HELLO!

Hello! Hello!
>>I am with you
>>and you are with me!

What a beautiful day
>>and how pretty it is,
>>now that the sun a shinning
>>and we are together again.

Yes, I feel it all,
>>all the beauty
>>and I am happy and thankful
>>to be apart of it.

Yes! Hello! Hello!
>>To all of you
>>and all of me
>>for love is all of round
>>and we
>>yes
>>all of us
>>are that love!

Yes! We are!
>>It is so wonderful
>>to be in love,
>>love
>>that is of us.

And most of all
>>it is so wonderful
>>to be with all of you
>>in God's love!

Amen.

w.j.scheck
santa ana
13 november 2000

EVERY MOMENT IS MY LAST

Now is the beginning
        of a new moment,
        a new realization,
        for now
        I am
        in the autumn
        of my years,
        and time is
        passing by.

How wonderful
        to realize this,
        for now
        I am
        with peace,
        and every moment
        is my
        last moment
        never
        to happen
        again,
        that
        I am
        approaching Glory,
        the Glory of the reunion of
        oneness!

Now!
        I can be
        what I am meant
        to be,
        and be in love
        with every moment,
        and be in
        GOD
        for
        eternity!

This is wonderful,
     a miracle
     for all the world struggles
     are over,
     I have done it all,
     and there is nothing
     new under the sun,
     and
     now
     I have left
     the earthly struggles
     and
     I am
     EXPERIENCING
     HEAVEN on earth!

And so it is
     with
     much
     thanks
     to
     GOD!

w.j. scheck
santa ana
14 november 2000

THE GLORY

Today is today
       with all its joys and Glory,
       it is a wonderful day to walk
       in the sunshine
       to be alive in LOVE.

Such a glorious day,
       and so much love and beauty
       that I am overwhelmed
       and speechless
       for all that you have given
       me
       my Dear Sweet Love,
       Thank You GOD
       for all of this,
       Thank You with all of
       my heart
       and
       LOVE
       for
       ALL
       of this!

For today
       I am living in the Glory
       of your sweet kind love
       and basking
       in the sunlight
       of your Glory

Think You
       again
       and
       again
       for
       ALL
       of
       THIS!

Amen!
w.j. scheck
santa ana
15 november 2000

About the Author

I am the author; but I am also you AND WE ARE APART OF GOD! Yes, I have history, I have been here and there, and I came here from another place, and I am a stranger in this strange land. I have done many ·things since coming here. In many ways, I am not one of you, for I came from a far off distance place. A place that you have never been and may never have the opportunity to go, unless you once again become one with the MIND of GOD!

When I came here, I forgot whom I was; and I went on a long journey finding myself in God. I have been to war, and seen many horrible atrocities! I am learned and have attained many degrees! Yet, I walked the earth not knowing whom I was. Then, I came to the realization that I was apart of the MIND of GOD. You may say how can this be, that he found out he was a part of the MIND of GOD how strange this sounds, but it is true! I could give you a list of the mundane things that I am; and some of you may be extremely impressed because I have done many significant things; but the biggest thing, which I have done is to find out that my mind is apart of the MIND of the ALL, of GOD, of ATUM; and this is where I originally came from when I came to this strange land. Yes, I walked into this body, and I will occupy it for a time until I return to the MIND of GOD and when this happens it will be joyful!

The author is available for personal and group spiritual counseling in addition to metaphysical training. He can be contacted via www.goldenlight.net and/or Golden Light Trust, 11151 Visalia Avenue, Lucerne Valley, California, 92356. Voice: 760-248-2100, Fax 760-248-2197.

Bibliography

Addington, Jack Ensign 1996
   The Hidden Mystery of the Bible. Marine del Ray, California:
   DeVoss & Company.

AMORC 1994
   Liber 777 - The Celestial Sanctum, San Jose, California,
   Rosicrucian Order, Amorc, Inc.

Cerullo, Morris 1995
   The Miracle Book. San Diego, California: Morris Cerullo World
   Evangelism.

Bardon, Franz 1993,
   Initiation Into Hermetics. Wuppertal, Germany: Dieter
Ruggeberg.

Chaney, E.C. 1966
   *"Man - Master of Destiny or Victim of Fate", Astara's Book of
Life 2, No 6.*

Choa Kok Sui 1990
   Pranic Healing. York Beach, Maine: Samuel Weiser, Inc.

Choa Kok Sui 1993
   Pranic Psychotherapy. York Beach, Maine: Samuel Weiser, Inc.

Elsbeth, Marguerite 1997
   Crystal Medicine. St. Paul, Minnesota: Llewellyn Publications.

Forshang Buddhism 1997
   The Unlimited Power of Your Innate Nature. Taipei, China:
   Forshang Buddhism   World Headquarters Publishing.

Gerber, Richard MD 1988
   Vibration Medicine. Santa Fe, New Mexico: Bear & Company.

Hinn, Benny 1994
   The Greatest Miracle. Orlando, Florida: Benny Hinn Media
   Ministries.

Kubose, Gyomay M. 1986

The Holy Bible 1978
Nashville, Tennessee: The Gideons International.

Wolfe, Amber 1997
In the Shadow of the Shaman. St. Paul, Minnesota: Llewellyn
Publications.

The Center Within. Union City, California. Heian International,
Inc.

Lamy, Lucie 1994
Egyptian Mysteries. New York, New York: Thames and Hudson.

Lansdowne, Zachary F. 1986
The Chakras & Esoteric Healing. York Beach, Maine: Samuel
Weiser, Inc.

Lubeck, Walter 1996
The Complete Reiki Handbook. Twin Lakes, Wisconsin: Lotus
Light-Shangri-La.

Motoyama, H. 1978
Science and the Evolution of Consciouness. Brookline,
Massachusetts: Autumn Press.

Rand, William Lee 1991
Reiki The Healing Touch. Southfield, Michigan: Vision
Publications

Reed, Henry 1988
Awakening your Psychic Powers. New York, New York: Harper
& Row, St.

Sanders, Pete A. Jr. 1989
You Are Pyschic - The Free Soul Method. New York, New York,
Fawcett Columbine, Batantine Books.

Smith, Mark 1997
Auras. St. Paul, Minnesota: Llewellyn Publications.

Szekely, Edmond Bordeaux 1978
>   *The Essene Gospel of Peace.* Nelson, B.C., Canada: International Biogenic Society.

Talbot, Michael 1991
>   *The Holographic Universe,* New York, New York: Harper Collins Publishers.